6. Enter your class ID code to join a class.

IF YOU HAVE A CLASS CODE FROM YOUR TEACHER

a. Enter your class code and click [**Next**]

b. Once you have joined a class, you will be able to use the Discussion Board and Email tools.

c. To enter this code later, choose **Join a Class**.

IF YOU DO NOT HAVE A CLASS CODE

a. If you do not have a class ID code, click [**Skip**]

b. You do not need a class ID code to use *iQ Online*.

c. To enter this code later, choose **Join a Class**.

7. Review registration information and click Log In. Then choose your book. Click **Activities** to begin using *iQ Online*.

IMPORTANT

- After you register, the next time you want to use *iQ Online*, go to www.iQOnlinePractice.com and log in with your email address and password.
- The online content can be used for 12 months from the date you register.
- For help, please contact customer service: cltsupport@oup.com.

WHAT IS iQ ONLINE ?

All new activities provide essential skills **practice** and support.

Vocabulary and Grammar **games** immerse you in the language and provide even more practice.

Authentic, engaging **videos** generate new ideas and opinions on the Unit Question.

Go to the Media Center to download or stream all **student book audio**.

Use the **Discussion Board** to discuss the Unit Question and more.

Email encourages communication with your teacher and classmates.

Automatic grading gives immediate feedback and tracks progress.

Progress Reports show what you have mastered and where you still need more practice.

SHAPING learning TOGETHER

We would like to acknowledge the teachers from all over the world who participated in the development process and review of the Q series.

Special thanks to our *Q: Skills for Success* Second Edition Topic Advisory Board

Shaker Ali Al-Mohammad, Buraimi University College, Oman; **Dr. Asmaa A. Ebrahim**, University of Sharjah, U.A.E.; **Rachel Batchilder**, College of the North Atlantic, Qatar; **Anil Bayir**, Izmir University, Turkey; **Flora Mcvay Bozkurt**, Maltepe University, Turkey; **Paul Bradley**, University of the Thai Chamber of Commerce Bangkok, Thailand; **Joan Birrell-Bertrand**, University of Manitoba, MB, Canada; **Karen E. Caldwell**, Zayed University, U.A.E.; **Nicole Hammond Carrasquel**, University of Central Florida, FL, U.S.; **Kevin Countryman**, Seneca College of Applied Arts & Technology, ON, Canada; **Julie Crocker**, Arcadia University, NS, Canada; **Marc L. Cummings**, Jefferson Community and Technical College, KY, U.S.; **Rachel DeSanto**, Hillsborough Community College Dale Mabry Campus, FL, U.S.; **Nilüfer Ertürkmen**, Ege University, Turkey; **Sue Fine**, Ras Al Khaimah Women's College (HCT), U.A.E.; **Amina Al Hashami**, Nizwa College of Applied Sciences, Oman; **Stephan Johnson**, Nagoya Shoka Daigaku, Japan; **Sean Kim**, Avalon, South Korea; **Gregory King**, Chubu Daigaku, Japan; **Seran Küçük**, Maltepe University, Turkey; **Jonee De Leon**, VUS, Vietnam; **Carol Lowther**, Palomar College, CA, U.S.; **Erin Harris-MacLead**, St. Mary's University, NS, Canada; **Angela Nagy**, Maltepe University, Turkey; **Huynh Thi Ai Nguyen**, Vietnam; **Daniel L. Paller**, Kinjo Gakuin University, Japan; **Jangyo Parsons**, Kookmin University, South Korea; **Laila Al Qadhi**, Kuwait University, Kuwait; **Josh Rosenberger**, English Language Institute University of Montana, MT, U.S.; **Nancy Schoenfeld**, Kuwait University, Kuwait; **Jenay Seymour**, Hongik University, South Korea; **Moon-young Son**, South Korea; **Matthew Taylor**, Kinjo Gakuin Daigaku, Japan; **Burcu Tezcan-Unal**, Zayed University, U.A.E.; **Troy Tucker**, Edison State College-Lee Campus, FL, U.S.; **Kris Vicca**, Feng Chia University, Taichung; **Jisook Woo**, Incheon University, South Korea; **Dunya Yenidunya**, Ege University, Turkey

UNITED STATES **Marcarena Aguilar**, North Harris College, TX; **Rebecca Andrade**, California State University North Ridge, CA; **Lesley Andrews**, Boston University, MA; **Deborah Anholt**, Lewis and Clark College, OR; **Robert Anzelde**, Oakton Community College, IL; **Arlys Arnold**, University of Minnesota, MN; **Marcia Arthur**, Renton Technical College, WA; **Renee Ashmeade**, Passaic County Community College, NJ; **Anne Bachmann**, Clackamas Community College, OR; **Lida Baker**, UCLA, CA; **Ron Balsamo**, Santa Rosa Junior College, CA; **Lori Barkley**, Portland State University, OR; **Eileen Barlow**, SUNY Albany, NY; **Sue Bartch**, Cuyahoga Community College, OH; **Lora Bates**, Oakton High School, VA; **Barbara Batra**, Nassau County Community College, NY; **Nancy Baum**, University of Texas at Arlington, TX; **Rebecca Beck**, Irvine Valley College, CA; **Linda Berendsen**, Oakton Community College, IL; **Jennifer Binckes Lee**, Howard Community College, MD; **Grace Bishop**, Houston Community College, TX; **Jean W. Bodman**, Union County College, NJ; **Virginia Bouchard**, George Mason University, VA; **Kimberley Briesch Sumner**, University of Southern California, CA; **Kevin Brown**, University of California, Irvine, CA; **Laura Brown**, Glendale Community College, CA; **Britta Burton**, Mission College, CA; **Allison L. Callahan**, Harold Washington College, IL; **Gabriela Cambiasso**, Harold Washington College, IL; **Jackie Campbell**, Capistrano Unified School District, CA; **Adele C. Camus**, George Mason University, VA; **Laura Chason**, Savannah College, GA; **Kerry Linder Catana**, Language Studies International, NY; **An Cheng**, Oklahoma State University, OK; **Carole Collins**, North Hampton Community College, PA; **Betty R. Compton**, Intercultural Communications College, HI; **Pamela Couch**, Boston University, MA; **Fernanda Crowe**, Intrax International Institute, CA; **Vicki Curtis**, Santa Cruz, CA; **Margo Czinski**, Washtenaw Community College, MI; **David Dahnke**, Lone Star College, TX; **Gillian M. Dale**, CA; **L. Dalgish**, Concordia College, MN; **Christopher Davis**, John Jay College, NY; **Sherry Davis**, Irvine University, CA; **Natalia de Cuba**, Nassau County Community College, NY; **Sonia Delgadillo**, Sierra College, CA; **Esmeralda Diriye**, Cypress College & Cal Poly, CA; **Marta O. Dmytrenko-Ahrabian**, Wayne State University, MI; **Javier Dominguez**, Central High School, SC; **Jo Ellen Downey-Greer**, Lansing Community College, MI; **Jennifer Duclos**, Boston University, MA; **Yvonne Duncan**, City College of San Francisco, CA; **Paul Dydman**, USC Language Academy, CA; **Anna Eddy**, University of Michigan-Flint, MI; **Zohan El-Gamal**, Glendale Community College, CA; **Jennie Farnell**, University of Connecticut, CT; **Susan Fedors**, Howard Community College, MD; **Valerie Fiechter**, Mission College, CA; **Ashley Fifer**, Nassau County Community College, NY; **Matthew Florence**, Intrax International Institute, CA; **Kathleen Flynn**, Glendale College, CA; **Elizabeth Fonsea**, Nassau County Community College, NY; **Eve Fonseca**, St. Louis Community College, MO; **Elizabeth Foss**, Washtenaw Community College, MI; **Duff C. Galda**, Pima Community College, AZ; **Christiane Galvani**, Houston Community College, TX; **Gretchen Gerber**, Howard Community College, MD; **Ray Gonzalez**, Montgomery College, MD; **Janet Goodwin**, University of California, Los Angeles, CA; **Alyona Gorokhova**, Grossmont College, CA; **John Graney**, Santa Fe College, FL; **Kathleen Green**, Central High School, AZ; **Nancy Hamadou**, Pima Community College-West Campus, AZ; **Webb Hamilton**, De Anza College, San Jose City College, CA; **Janet Harclerode**, Santa Monica Community College, CA; **Sandra Hartmann**, Language and Culture Center, TX; **Kathy Haven**, Mission College, CA; **Roberta Hendrick**, Cuyahoga Community College, OH; **Ginny Heringer**, Pasadena City College, CA; **Adam Henricksen**, University of Maryland, MD; **Carolyn Ho**, Lone Star College-CyFair, TX; **Peter Hoffman**, LaGuardia Community College, NY; **Linda Holden**, College of Lake County, IL; **Jana Holt**, Lake Washington Technical College, WA; **Antonio Iccarino**, Boston University, MA; **Gail Ibele**, University of Wisconsin, WI; **Nina Ito**, American Language Institute, CSU Long Beach, CA; **Linda Jensen**, UCLA, CA; **Lisa Jurkowitz**, Pima Community College, CA; **Mandy Kama**, Georgetown University, Washington, DC; **Stephanie Kasuboski**, Cuyahoga Community College, OH; **Chigusa Katoku**, Mission College, CA; **Sandra Kawamura**, Sacramento City College, CA; **Gail Kellersberger**, University of Houston-Downtown, TX; **Jane Kelly**, Durham Technical Community College, NC; **Maryanne Kildare**, Nassau County Community College, NY; **Julie Park Kim**, George Mason University, VA; **Kindra Kinyon**, Los Angeles Trade-Technical College, CA; **Matt Kline**, El Camino College, CA; **Lisa Kovacs-Morgan**, University of California, San Diego, CA; **Claudia Kupiec**, DePaul University, IL; **Renee La Rue**, Lone Star College-Montgomery, TX; **Janet Langon**, Glendale College, CA; **Lawrence Lawson**, Palomar College, CA; **Rachele Lawton**, The Community College of Baltimore County, MD; **Alice Lee**, Richland College, TX; **Esther S. Lee**, CSUF & Mt. SAC, CA; **Cherie Lenz-Hackett**, University of Washington, WA; **Joy Leventhal**, Cuyahoga Community College, OH; **Alice Lin**, UCI Extension, CA; **Monica Lopez**, Cerritos College, CA; **Dustin Lovell**, FLS International Marymount College, CA; **Carol Lowther**, Palomar College, CA; **Candace Lynch-Thompson**, North Orange County Community College District, CA; **Thi Thi Ma**, City College of San Francisco, CA; **Steve Mac Isaac**, USC Long Academy, CA; **Denise Maduli-Williams**, City College of San Francisco, CA; **Eileen Mahoney**, Camelback High School, AZ; **Naomi Mardock**, MCC-Omaha, NE; **Brigitte Maronde**, Harold Washington College, IL; **Marilyn Marquis**, Laposita College CA; **Doris Martin**, Glendale Community College; Pasadena City College, CA; **Keith Maurice**, University of Texas at Arlington, TX; **Nancy Mayer**, University of Missouri-St. Louis, MO; **Aziah McNamara**, Kansas State University, KS; **Billie McQuillan**, Education Heights, MN; **Karen Merritt**, Glendale Union High School District, AZ; **Holly Milkowart**, Johnson County Community College, KS; **Eric Moyer**, Intrax International Institute, CA; **Gino Muzzatti**, Santa Rosa Junior College, CA; **Sandra Navarro**, Glendale Community College, CA; **Than Nyeinkhin**, ELAC, PCC, CA; **William Nedrow**, Triton College, IL; **Eric Nelson**, University of Minnesota, MN; **Than Nyeinkhin**, ELAC, PCC, CA; **Fernanda Ortiz**, Center for English as a Second Language at the University of Arizona, AZ; **Rhony Ory**, Ygnacio Valley High School, CA; **Paul Parent**, Montgomery College, MD; **Dr. Sumeeta Patnaik**, Marshall University, WV; **Oscar Pedroso**, Miami Dade College, FL; **Robin Persiani**, Sierra College, CA; **Patricia Prenz-Belkin**, Hostos Community College, NY; **Suzanne Powell**, University of Louisville, KY; **Jim Ranalli**, Iowa State University, IA; **Toni R. Randall**, Santa Monica College, CA; **Vidya Rangachari**, Mission College, CA; **Elizabeth Rasmussen**, Northern Virginia Community College, VA; **Lara Ravitch**, Truman College, IL;

Industry, Vietnam; **Do Thi Thanh Nhan**, Hanoi University, Vietnam; **Dale Kazuo Nishi**, Aoyama English Conversation School, Japan; **Huynh Thi Ai Nguyen**, Vietnam; **Dongshin Oh**, YBM PLS, South Korea; **Keiko Okada**, Dokkyo Daigaku, Japan; **Louise Ohashi**, Shukutoku University, Japan; **Yongjun Park**, Sangji University, South Korea; **Donald Patnaude**, Ajarn Donald's English Language Services, Thailand; **Virginia Peng**, Ritsumeikan University, Japan; **Suangkanok Piboonthamnont**, Rajamangala University of Technology, Thailand; **Simon Pitcher**, Business English Teaching Services, Japan; **John C. Probert**, New Education Worldwide, Thailand; **Do Thi Hoa Quyen**, Ton Duc Thang University, Vietnam; **John P. Racine**, Dokkyo University, Japan; **Kevin Ramsden**, Kyoto University of Foreign Studies, Japan; **Luis Rappaport**, Cung Thieu Nha Ha Noi, Vietnam; **Lisa Reshad**, Konan Daigaku Hyogo, Japan; **Peter Riley**, Taisho University, Japan; **Thomas N. Robb**, Kyoto Sangyo University, Japan; **Rory Rosszell**, Meiji Daigaku, Japan; **Maria Feti Rosyani**, Universitas Kristen Indonesia, Indonesia; **Greg Rouault**, Konan University, Japan; **Chris Ruddenklau**, Kindai University, Japan; **Hans-Gustav Schwartz**, Thailand; **Mary-Jane Scott**, Soongsil University, South Korea; **Dara Sheahan**, Seoul National University, South Korea; **James Sherlock**, A.P.W. Angthong, Thailand; **Prof. Shieh**, Minghsin University of Science & Technology, Xinfeng; **Yuko Shimizu**, Ritsumeikan University, Japan; **Suzila Mohd Shukor**, Universiti Sains Malaysia, Malaysia; **Stephen E. Smith**, Mahidol University, Thailand; **Moon-young Son**, South Korea; **Seunghee Son**, Anyang University, South Korea; **Mi-young Song**, Kyungwon University, South Korea; **Lisa Sood**, VUS, BIS, Vietnam; **Jason Stewart**, Taejon International Language School, South Korea; **Brian A. Stokes**, Korea University, South Korea; **Mulder Su**, Shih-Chien University, Kaohsiung; **Yoomi Suh**, English Plus, South Korea; **Yun-Fang Sun**, Wenzao Ursuline College of Languages, Kaohsiung; **Richard Swingle**, Kansai Gaidai University, Japan; **Sanford Taborn**, Kinjo Gakuin Daigaku, Japan; **Mamoru Takahashi**, Akita Prefectural University, Japan; **Tran Hoang Tan**, School of International Training, Vietnam; **Takako Tanaka**, Doshisha University, Japan; **Jeffrey Taschner**, American University Alumni Language Center, Thailand; **Matthew Taylor**, Kinjo Gakuin Daigaku, Japan; **Michael Taylor**, International Pioneers School, Thailand; **Kampanart Thammaphati**, Wattana Wittaya Academy, Thailand; **Tran Duong The**, Sao Mai Language Center, Vietnam; **Tran Dinh Tho**, Duc Tri Secondary School, Vietnam; **Huynh Thi Anh Thu**, Nhatrang College of Culture Arts and Tourism, Vietnam; **Peter Timmins**, Peter's English School, Japan; **Fumie Togano**, Hosei Daini High School, Japan; **F. Sigmund Topor**, Keio University Language School, Japan; **Tu Trieu**, Rise VN, Vietnam; **Yen-Cheng Tseng**, Chang-Jung Christian University, Tainan; **Pei-Hsuan Tu**, National Cheng Kung University, Tainan City; **Hajime Uematsu**, Hirosaki University, Japan; **Rachel Um**, Mok-dong Oedae English School, South Korea; **David Underhill**, EEExpress, Japan; **Ben Underwood**, Kugenuma High School, Japan; **Siriluck Usaha**, Sripatum University, Thailand; **Tyas Budi Utami**, Indonesia; **Nguyen Thi Van**, Far East International School, Vietnam; **Stephan Van Eycken**, Kosei Gakuen Girls High School, Japan; **Zisa Velasquez**, Taihu International School/Semarang International School, China/Indonesia; **Jeffery Walter**, Sangji University, South Korea; **Bill White**, Kinki University, Japan; **Yohanes De Deo Widyastoko**, Xaverius Senior High School, Indonesia; **Dylan Williams**, SNU, South Korea; **Jisuk Woo**, Ichean University, South Korea; **Greg Chung-Hsien Wu**, Providence University, Taichung; **Xun Xiaoming**, BLCU, China; **Hui-Lien Yeh**, Chai Nan University of Pharmacy and Science, Tainan; **Sittiporn Yodnil**, Huachiew Chalermprakiet University, Thailand; **Shamshul Helmy Zambahari**, Universiti Teknologi Malaysia, Malaysia; **Ming-Yuli**, Chang Jung Christian University, Tainan; **Aimin Fadhlee bin Mahmud Zuhodi**, Kuala Terengganu Science School, Malaysia;

TURKEY **Shirley F. Akis**, American Culture Association/Fomara; **Gül Akkoç**, Boğaziçi University; **Seval Akmeşe**, Haliç University; **Ayşenur Akyol**, Ege University; **Ayşe Umut Aribaş**, Beykent University; **Gökhan Asan**, Kapadokya Vocational College; **Hakan Asan**, Kapadokya Vocational College; **Julia Asan**, Kapadokya Vocational College; **Azarvan Atac**, Piri Reis University; **Nur Babat**, Kapadokya Vocational College; **Feyza Balakbabalar**, Kadir Has University; **Gözde Balikçi**, Beykent University; **Deniz Balım**, Haliç University; **Asli Başdoğan**, Kadir Has University; **Ayla Bayram**, Kapadokya Vocational College; **Pinar Bilgiç**, Kadir Has University; **Kenan Bozkurt**, Kapadokya Vocational College; **Yonca Bozkurt**, Ege University; **Frank Carr**, Piri Reis; **Mengü Noyan Çengel**, Ege University; **Elif Doğan**, Ege University; **Natalia Donmez**, 29 Mayis Üniversite; **Nalan Emirsoy**, Kadir Has University; **Ayşe Engin**, Kadir Has University; **Ayhan Gedikbaş**, Ege University; **Gülşah Gençer**, Beykent University; **Seyit Ömer Gök**, Gediz University; **Tuğba Gök**, Gediz University; **İlkay Gökçe**, Ege University; **Zeynep Birinci Guler**, Maltepe University; **Neslihan Güler**, Kadir Has University; **Sircan Gümüş**,

Kadir Has University; **Nesrin Gündoğu**, T.C. Piri Reis University; **Tanju Gurpinar**, Piri Reis University; **Selin Gurturk**, Piri Reis University; **Neslihan Gurutku**, Piri Reis University; **Roger Hewitt**, Maltepe University; **Nilüfer İbrahimoğlu**, Beykent University; **Nevin Kaftelen**, Kadir Has University; **Sultan Kalin**, Kapadokya Vocational College; **Sema Kaplan Karabina**, Anadolu University; **Eray Kara**, Giresun University; **Beylü Karayazgan**, Ege University; **Darren Kelso**, Piri Reis University; **Trudy Kittle**, Kapadokya Vocational College; **Şaziye Konaç**, Kadir Has University; **Güneş Korkmaz**, Kapadokya Vocational College; **Robert Ledbury**, Izmir University of Economics; **Ashley Lucas**, Maltepe University; **Bülent Nedium Uça**, Dogus University; **Murat Nurlu**, Ege University; **Mollie Owens**, Kadir Has University; **Oya Özağaç**, Boğaziçi University; **Funda Özcan**, Ege University; **İlkay Özdemir**, Ege University; **Ülkü Öztürk**, Gediz University; **Cassondra Puls**, Anadolu University; **Yelda Sarikaya**, Cappadocia Vocational College; **Müge Şekercioğlu**, Ege University; **Melis Senol**, Canakkale Onsekiz Mart University, The School of Foreign Languages; **Patricia Sümer**, Kadir Has University; **Rex Surface**, Beykent University; **Mustafa Torun**, Kapadokya Vocational College; **Tansel Üstünloğlu**, Ege University; **Fatih Yücel**, Beykent University; **Şule Yüksel**, Ege University;

THE MIDDLE EAST **Amina Saif Mohammed Al Hashamia**, Nizwa College of Applied Sciences, Oman; **Jennifer Baran**, Kuwait University, Kuwait; **Phillip Chappells**, GEMS Modern Academy, U.A.E.; **Sharon Ruth Devaneson**, Ibri College of Technology, Oman; **Hanaa El-Deeb**, Canadian International College, Egypt; **Yvonne Eaton**, Community College of Qatar, Qatar; **Brian Gay**, Sultan Qaboos University, Oman; **Gail Al Hafidh**, Sharjah Women's College (HCT), U.A.E.; **Jonathan Hastings**, American Language Center, Jordan; **Laurie Susan Hilu**, English Language Centre, University of Bahrain, Bahrain; **Abraham Irannezhad**, Mehre Aval, Iran; **Kevin Kempe**, CNA-Q, Qatar; **Jill Newby James**, University of Nizwa; **Mary Kay Klein**, American University of Sharjah, U.A.E.; **Sian Khoury**, Fujairah Women's College (HCT), U.A.E.; **Hussein Dehghan Manshadi**, Farhang Pajooh & Jaam-e-Jam Language School, Iran; **Jessica March**, American University of Sharjah, U.A.E.; **Neil McBeath**, Sultan Qaboos University, Oman; **Sandy McDonagh**, Abu Dhabi Men's College (HCT), U.A.E.; **Rob Miles**, Sharjah Women's College (HCT), U.A.E.; **Michael Kevin Neumann**, Al Ain Men's College (HCT), U.A.E.;

LATIN AMERICA **Aldana Aguirre**, Argentina; **Claudia Almeida**, Coordenação de Idiomas, Brazil; **Cláudia Arias**, Brazil; **Maria de los Angeles Barba**, FES Acatlan UNAM, Mexico; **Lilia Barrios**, Universidad Autónoma de Tamaulipas, Mexico; **Adán Beristain**, UAEM, Mexico; **Ricardo Böck**, Manoel Ribas, Brazil; **Edson Braga**, CNA, Brazil; **Marli Buttelli**, Mater et Magistra, Brazil; **Alessandra Campos**, Inova Centro de Linguas, Brazil; **Priscila Catta Preta Ribeiro**, Brazil; **Gustavo Cestari**, Access International School, Brazil; **Walter D'Alessandro**, Virginia Language Center, Brazil; **Lilian De Gennaro**, Argentina; **Mônica De Stefani**, Quality Centro de Idiomas, Brazil; **Julio Alejandro Flores**, BUAP, Mexico; **Mirian Freire**, CNA Vila Guilherme, Brazil; **Francisco Garcia**, Colegio Lestonnac de San Angel, Mexico; **Miriam Giovanardi**, Brazil; **Darlene Gonzalez Miy**, ITESM CCV, Mexico; **Maria Laura Grimaldi**, Argentina; **Luz Dary Guzmán**, IMPAHU, Colombia; **Carmen Koppe**, Brazil; **Monica Krutzler**, Brazil; **Marcus Murilo Lacerda**, Seven Idiomas, Brazil; **Nancy Lake**, CEL-LEP, Brazil; **Cris Lazzerini**, Brazil; **Sandra Luna**, Argentina; **Ricardo Luvisan**, Brazil; **Jorge Murilo Menezes**, ACBEU, Brazil; **Monica Navarro**, Instituto Cultural A. C., Mexico; **Joacyr Oliveira**, Faculdades Metropolitanas Unidas and Summit School for Teachers, Brazil; **Ayrton Cesar Oliveira de Araujo**, E&A English Classes, Brazil; **Ana Laura Oriente**, Seven Idiomas, Brazil; **Adelia Peña Clavel**, CELE UNAM, Mexico; **Beatriz Pereira**, Summit School, Brazil; **Miguel Perez**, Instituto Cultural, Mexico; **Cristiane Perone**, Associação Cultura Inglesa, Brazil; **Pamela Claudia Pogré**, Colegio Integral Caballito / Universidade de Flores, Argentina; **Dalva Prates**, Brazil; **Marianne Rampaso**, Iowa Idiomas, Brazil; **Daniela Rutolo**, Instituto Superior Cultural Británico, Argentina; **Maione Sampaio**, Maione Carrijo Consultoria em Inglês Ltda, Brazil; **Elaine Santesso**, TS Escola de Idiomas, Brazil; **Camila Francisco Santos**, UNS Idiomas, Brazil; **Lucia Silva**, Cooplem Idiomas, Brazil; **Maria Adela Sorzio**, Instituto Superior Santa Cecilia, Argentina; **Elcio Souza**, Unibero, Brazil; **Willie Thomas**, Rainbow Idiomas, Brazil; **Sandra Villegas**, Instituto Humberto de Paolis, Argentina; **John Whelan**, La Universidad Nacional Autonoma de Mexico, Mexico

CONTENTS

NOTE TAKING	▶	using a chart to organize notes about main ideas
LISTENING	▶	listening for main ideas
VOCABULARY	▶	understanding meaning from context
GRAMMAR	▶	gerunds and infinitives
PRONUNCIATION	▶	syllable stress
SPEAKING	▶	checking for understanding

UNIT QUESTION

What makes a good leader?

A Discuss these questions with your classmates.

1. Have you ever been a leader? For example, have you ever been in charge of a group at school or been the captain of a sports team? If so, what challenges did you face as a leader?

2. Think of a leader you admire. What makes this person a good leader?

3. Look at the photo. Identify the leader. What qualities make this person an effective leader?

UNIT
OBJECTIVE ▶▶▶▶ Listen to a report and a lecture and gather information
and ideas to give a presentation about how to be an
effective leader.

◉ B Listen to *The Q Classroom* online. Then answer these questions.

1. Yuna feels that leaders should act more responsibly when they have power. Do you agree? Why or why not?

2. Felix says that becoming a leader makes a person's life difficult in some ways. Do you agree? If so, in what ways do you think becoming a leader would make a person's life more difficult?

 C Go online to watch a video about a creative business leader. Then check your comprehension.

VIDEO VOCABULARY

CEO *(n.)* chief executive officer (the person with the highest rank in a business)

perk *(n.)* something extra you receive in addition to your wages for doing a particular job

puts himself at arm's length *(idm.)* avoids having a close relationship with someone

walks the walk *(idm.)* acts in a way that shows people you are really good at what you do, and not just good at talking about it

 **D Go to the Online Discussion Board to discuss the Unit Question with your classmates.**

3

E Think about some important characteristics of a leader. Check (✓) the three characteristics you think are most important. Compare your answers with a partner.

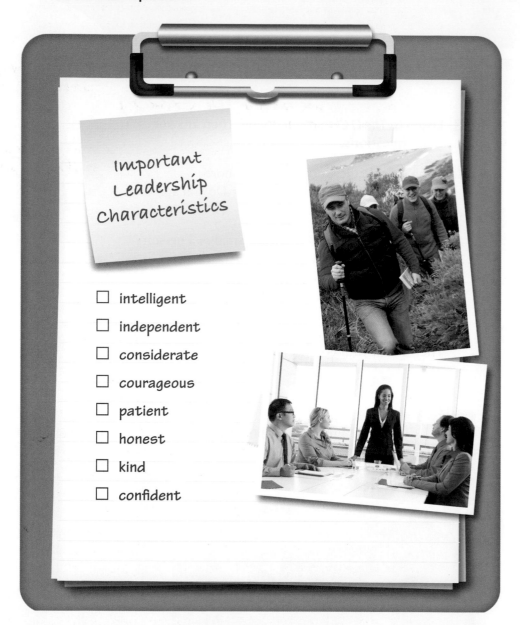

Important Leadership Characteristics

☐ intelligent

☐ independent

☐ considerate

☐ courageous

☐ patient

☐ honest

☐ kind

☐ confident

F Discuss these questions in a group.

1. What kinds of people become leaders?

2. What are some characteristics of people who are not good leaders?

3. "A group of sheep led by a lion would defeat a group of lions led by a sheep" is an Arabic proverb. What do you think it means?

Charts are a useful way to organize your notes on a presentation. Using a chart to list main ideas can help you understand how a presentation is organized and can help you identify the speaker's most important points.

To organize your notes about main ideas, divide your page into two columns. Use the left column to show how the presentation is organized. Use the right column to write down the main ideas. You can also write any key words or phrases that support each main idea.

Look at the example below from Activity A. The student uses the left column to show the topics in a text and the right column to show the main ideas and key phrases.

Topic: Motivating teams	Main ideas and key phrases
First way	Make expectations clear
	- gives team a goal

A. Read this section of a talk about motivating team members. Circle what you think are the main ideas. Underline any key words or phrases that support each main idea.

If you are a leader, then you know that highly motivated people do better work than people who are discouraged, tired, or just unenthusiastic. But how can you keep a team excited over the long haul? How can you motivate them to do their best? Those aren't easy questions, but here are three simple ways to start. First of all, make sure you're communicating your expectations clearly. When you explain what you expect, you're providing your team members with a specific goal. And this will help your team focus their energy and efforts on what is important. Beyond that, make sure to provide your whole team with feedback that will help them improve. Helpful feedback makes it easier for us to learn and develop, and it also helps us to identify and correct problems before they get too big. Lastly, remember to reward good work. Don't just be a critic. Rewards can be anything from a "thank you" to a party, a pay raise, or even a day off. Be creative, and don't be cheap. Make sure your team knows when they've done well. They'll get excited when they know a reward is on its way, and they'll feel like their hard work is actually paying off.

B. Complete the chart with the main ideas and the supporting words and phrases you identified in Activity A. Compare your notes with a partner. Then take turns coming up with your own examples of each way to motivate team members.

Topic: Motivating teams	Main ideas and key phrases
First way	Make expectations clear - gives team a goal -
Second way	
Third way	

C. Go online for more practice using a chart to organize notes about main ideas.

LISTENING

LISTENING 1 | Best of Both Worlds?

You are going to listen to a report that discusses the challenges of being a friend's boss. As you listen to the report, gather information and ideas about what makes a good leader.

PREVIEW THE LISTENING

Can a boss be a friend?

A. **PREVIEW** Discuss this question with a partner: If someone becomes the boss of a friend, what difficulties do you think the friends will face?

B. **VOCABULARY** Read aloud these words from Listening 1. Check (✓) the ones you know. Use a dictionary to define any new or unknown words. Then discuss with a partner how the words will relate to the unit.

acknowledge *(v.)* 🔑	exemplify *(v.)*	negotiate *(v.)*
address *(v.)* 🔑	expert *(n.)* 🔑	outline *(v.)* 🔑
aspect *(n.)* 🔑	favoritism *(n.)*	potential *(n.)* 🔑
criticism *(n.)* 🔑	issue *(n.)* 🔑	staff *(n.)* 🔑

🔑 Oxford 3000™ words

 C. Go online to listen and practice your pronunciation.

WORK WITH THE LISTENING

🔊 **A.** **LISTEN AND TAKE NOTES** Listen to the report and take notes on the experiences each woman had when she became a friend's boss. Write the main ideas and key phrases you hear.

Topic: Being a friend's boss	Main ideas and key phrases
Ginny Pitcher's experiences	
Carly Drum's experiences	
Tory Delany's experiences	

B. Use your notes to match each person with a step she took when she became a friend's boss.

____ 1. Ginny Pitcher

____ 2. Carly Drum

____ 3. Tory Delany

a. She worked with her friend to develop a plan for separating work from business.

b. She warned any employees who came to work late more than once.

c. She acknowledged there would be a change in the friendship and talked with her friend about the challenges they might face.

C. Read the statements. Write *T* (true) or *F* (false). Then correct the false statements.

____ 1. It is important to bring personal issues into business relationships.

_____

____ 2. A manager must outline for a friend what is expected at work.

_____

____ 3. A good boss should always try to show favoritism.

_____

____ 4. The key to working with friends is developing rules and boundaries.

_____

D. Read the sentences. Then listen again. Circle the correct answers.

1. What did Kate Massey do when her friend Ginny Pitcher offered her a job?
   a. She rejected the offer.
   b. She hesitated before accepting the offer.
   c. She quickly accepted the offer.

2. After working together for a year, what happened to the relationship between Kate Massey and Ginny Pitcher?
   a. They became roommates.
   b. They were no longer friends.
   c. Their friendship was still strong.

3. According to Ginny Pitcher, what is one benefit of hiring close friends?
   a. You already know their personalities.
   b. You know that you can trust them.
   c. You know if they are qualified for the job.

4. When Carly Drum hired four trusted friends, what did one of her friends do?
   a. She expected to receive more money.
   b. She allowed personal problems to affect her work.
   c. She stopped coming to work and soon quit.

5. What happened when Tory Delany became the manager at a restaurant in Manhattan?
   a. She had to fire a friend.
   b. She managed some friends.
   c. She hired her best friend.

6. What does Tory Delany say will happen if a manager does not enforce rules and structure with employees?
   a. The manager's team will fall apart.
   b. The manager will lose his or her job.
   c. The manager's employees will quit.

E. VOCABULARY Here are some words from Listening 1. Complete each sentence with the correct word.

acknowledge (v.)	criticism (n.)	favoritism (n.)	outline (v.)
address (v.)	exemplify (v.)	issue (n.)	potential (n.)
aspect (n.)	expert (n.)	negotiate (v.)	staff (n.)

1. Good employees take _____ well. They hear what they are doing wrong, and they make appropriate changes to their work.

2. Bob showed _____ when he promoted Hwa-jeong. They are friends, so Hwa-jeong got the job instead of Laura.

3. I _____ that I made a mistake on the report. I take responsibility, and I will correct it.

4. The new employee has a lot of _____. She knows a lot about our business. I'm sure she'll be promoted soon.

5. The new plan gives employees more vacation time. That's one _____ of the plan I really like!

6. Tom is a(n) _____ at this computer program. He worked with it for many years, and he teaches classes about it.

7. The manager told the _____ that an important customer was pleased with their work. Everyone thought that was great news.

8. I know we don't agree on this subject, but I'm sure we can _____ a solution that we both like.

9. The project is very complex, so I'll _____ the basic problems we are trying to fix.

10. I'd like to _____ one of the main questions that people ask in meetings. Together we can find an answer.

11. David and Ernesto are always on time, and they work well with others. I think they _____ good employees.

12. We need to settle this _____. Arguing about it will not help us solve the problem.

 **F.** Go online for more practice with the vocabulary.

 ## SAY WHAT YOU THINK

Discuss the questions in a group.

1. What do you think are the main advantages of hiring a friend?

2. If you were a small business owner, would you consider hiring your closest friend to work for you? Why or why not?

3. If your closest friend became your boss, how would this affect your relationship? How do you think your friend might change?

When listening to a presentation, it is difficult to remember every piece of information you hear. Instead of trying to remember every detail, it is more important to identify the speaker's **main ideas**. These are the most important ideas that the speaker wants you to understand and remember.

A speaker often states the main idea as part of the introduction. Here are some signal phrases used to introduce main ideas.

> Today <u>we'll focus on</u> . . .
> This morning <u>we'll consider</u> . . .
> Today <u>I'm going to talk about</u> . . .
> For today's lecture, <u>we're going to look at</u> . . .

Main ideas are often repeated or rephrased during a presentation, especially at the end.

After you listen and take notes, review your notes. Notice which ideas are repeated or described in greater detail. This will help you decide what the main ideas are.

A. Read the introduction to each presentation. Circle the option that best describes the main idea of each presentation.

1. For most people, business meetings are boring, but they don't have to be that way. Today I'm going to give you a few tips on how to run an effective business meeting. Although not every tip might work for you, meetings don't have to put everyone in the room to sleep.
   a. Business meetings are often boring because they're too long and waste too much time.
   b. Business meetings are often boring, but there are ways to make them worthwhile.
   c. Business meetings are often boring, so we should find ways to eliminate them.

2. Hiring the right employees can be a real challenge. Many managers add a new person to their staff who is not a good choice. Let's consider some techniques to evaluate potential employees and explore ways to successfully pick the best people to hire.
   a. Many people hire employees for the wrong reasons. Soon they regret their hiring decisions.
   b. It is important that managers learn to recognize that someone is not a good hiring choice.
   c. Hiring employees can be difficult, but this presentation will teach skills for choosing the best possible employees.

3. There are many job-finding tools available online. For instance, some websites tell job searchers about positions that are available, while others give tips on writing a résumé or answering questions in a job interview. Today I'd like to focus on how to make the best use of these online tools. Online job resources are valuable, but they won't help us much if we don't know the best ways to use them.

   a. Job searchers should learn how to answer interview questions and write résumés.

   b. Job searchers should learn how to use online job-finding tools effectively.

   c. Job searchers should go online to find out about available jobs.

B. Listen to a short presentation. As you listen, take notes in the chart.

Topic	
Most important factor	
First characteristic mentioned	
Second characteristic mentioned	
Last characteristic mentioned	

 C. Go online for more practice with listening for main ideas.

LISTENING 2 | Myths of Effective Leadership

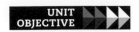

You are going to listen to a lecture from the Center for Creative Leadership, an organization dedicated to helping executives by providing them with the information and skills they need to lead well and overcome common challenges. As you listen to the lecture, gather information and ideas about what makes a good leader.

PREVIEW THE LISTENING

A. **PREVIEW** In this lecture, the speaker presents some of the negative ways in which successful executives may change. List two ways that you think people tend to change negatively when they become leaders.

1. _____

2. _____

B. **VOCABULARY** Read aloud these words from Listening 2. Check (✓) the ones you know. Use a dictionary to define any new or unknown words. Then discuss with a partner how the words will relate to the unit.

advance *(v.)* 🔑	effective *(adj.)* 🔑	style *(n.)* 🔑
assess *(v.)*	ethical *(adj.)*	title *(n.)* 🔑
capable *(adj.)* 🔑	executive *(n.)* 🔑	
contact *(n.)* 🔑	perspective *(n.)* 🔑	

🔑 Oxford 3000™ words

 **C.** Go online to listen and practice your pronunciation.

WORK WITH THE LISTENING

A. **LISTEN AND TAKE NOTES** Listen to the lecture and take notes in the charts.

Actions of ineffective leaders	Main ideas and key phrases
First example	
Second example	
Third example	

Advice for leaders	Main ideas and key phrases
First piece of advice	
Second piece of advice	
Third piece of advice	

B. Use your notes to answer the questions.

1. According to a study by the Center for Creative Leadership, how do many powerful executives see themselves?

   _____

2. What do many powerful executives think about people who disagree with them?

   _____

3. How do employees begin to react to these executives?

   _____

C. Read the statements. Then listen again. Write _T_ (true) or _F_ (false). Then correct the false statements.

_____ 1. Many executives forget the skills that helped them become successful.

   _____

_____ 2. An effective executive must know the difference between power and leadership.

   _____

_____ 3. A study shows that most executives respect employees who disagree with them.

   _____

_____ 4. Many executives begin to believe they are more powerful than they really are.

   _____

_____ 5. It is impossible to learn the skills necessary for effective leadership.

_____

_____ 6. To become an effective leader, you must view yourself through the eyes of your team members.

_____

D. Read the advice on leadership. Check (✓) the advice you think the speaker would agree with.

☐ 1. When team members disagree with you, ask some questions and take time to consider their perspectives.

☐ 2. Encourage your team members to ask questions about your decisions and plans.

☐ 3. Instead of personal meetings, announce major business decisions and plans by email or video.

☐ 4. Invite team members to fill out anonymous feedback forms about your performance and your leadership style.

☐ 5. Keep your contact with team members brief. If they have concerns or complaints, encourage them to speak with your assistant.

E. Read the examples of decisions made by leaders. Based on the information in the lecture, do they demonstrate effective or ineffective leadership? Write _E_ (effective) or _I_ (ineffective). Then discuss your choices with a partner.

_____ 1. The president of Linear Electronics, James Yoo, hires all managers from outside his company. He doesn't believe in promoting existing team members to management positions.

_____ 2. Reggie Silva, head coach of the Tower University baseball team, has breakfast with players individually each month to find out how they are doing.

_____ 3. Restaurant owner Claudia Tavares placed an "idea box" near the door of her restaurant. She checks it each week for thoughts from her customers.

_____ 4. Daniel Lisa was elected president of his university's engineering club. He assigned people who voted for him to all the advisory board positions.

_____ 5. Edgar Molina, vice president of Trident Bank, tries to read several leadership books each year.

_____ 6. Governor Patricia Landon keeps her office door open so team members can come in and talk whenever they want to.

_____ 7. The head of the English Literature Department, Coleen Zhang, believes it is much more efficient to make most departmental decisions on her own. Involving others in the decision-making process takes too long.

F. **VOCABULARY** Here are some words from Listening 2. Complete each sentence with the correct word.

advance (v.)	contact (n.)	executive (n.)	title (n.)
assess (v.)	effective (adj.)	perspective (n.)	
capable (adj.)	ethical (adj.)	style (n.)	

1. We need to hire a more _____ office assistant. The current assistant doesn't have enough experience and isn't highly skilled.

2. My management _____ is very different from Roger's. I prefer to lead by example. He prefers to give detailed instructions to employees.

3. I'm nervous about the meeting with my manager next Monday. She is going to _____ my performance for this year.

4. Blake joined the company in 2000. Within five years he was able to _____ to the position of vice president.

5. Please tell me what you think about this design. I'm interested in hearing your _____ on it.

6. Anne knows a lot of people in our industry. She has a good business _____ at the London office who can help us.

7. I am concerned that our company is not making _____ decisions. Our factory creates more pollution and waste than it needs to.

8. We created a plan to save the company. Unfortunately, it was not as _____ as we had hoped, and the company was forced to close last month.

9. I called her *Mrs. Rodgers*, but later I learned that her _____ is actually *Doctor*.

10. Emma only recently started working for the company, but her goal is to become a(n) _____ there someday. I think she will make a good manager.

 **G.** Go online for more practice with the vocabulary.

H. Go online to listen to *Are Leaders Born or Made?* and check your comprehension.

 SAY WHAT YOU THINK

A. Discuss the questions in a group.

1. The speaker states that leadership and power are not the same. What do you think are some differences between leadership and power?

2. According to the lecture, some successful executives begin to "blur the lines" between leadership and power. They act as if leadership and power are the same thing. Why do you think this happens?

B. Think about the unit video, Listening 1, and Listening 2 as you discuss the questions.

1. Power can affect relationships and individuals in a negative way. What are some positive effects power may have?

2. Both Listenings offer advice to bosses. Which advice do you think is the most valuable? Is there any advice that you disagree with? Why?

Vocabulary Skill	Understanding meaning from context

One way to figure out the meaning of a word is from the **context** of the sentence it is in. Use the words around the unknown word to help you understand the new word.

> She started as a coat checker at Maggie's Place . . . and, after a series of promotions, eventually became general manager.

The speaker mentions that Ms. Delany "started" in one position and "eventually became general manager." These words describe making progress in a company over time. The context tells you that *promotion* means receiving a higher position or a more important job.

It also helps to consider the presentation as a whole, not just one sentence.

> Knowing someone will fit in doesn't alleviate other problems. Carly Drum had hired four trusted friends to work at her family's executive search firm . . . One of them had great potential but was bringing her personal problems to the office. It was affecting her work.

The speaker uses several sentences to describe a problem that developed when Carly Drum hired a friend. From this context, you may be able to figure out that to *alleviate* problems means to solve, correct, or remove the problems.

A. Listen to the sentences. Use the context to match each bold word with its definition.

____ 1. The job didn't pay very well, but I loved the office and my co-workers. It was a great **environment** to work in.

____ 2. It's impossible to **function** well when you don't get along with your co-workers. I can't work in a situation like that.

____ 3. I'm sure you can **resolve** the conflict with your co-worker if you listen to each other's opinions.

____ 4. James has great **aptitude**, but he needs more training. In a year or so, he'll probably be our best programmer.

____ 5. The members of Emily's group are experienced and talented. Besides, they **exhibit** great teamwork.

a. natural ability to do something

b. the conditions that affect a person's behavior and development

c. to work in the correct way

d. to find an acceptable solution to a problem

e. to show or display

B. Listen to excerpts from Listening 1 and Listening 2. Circle the correct answers.

1. **In charge of** probably means ____.
   a. meeting with
   b. working with
   c. having responsibility over

2. **Interaction** probably means ____.
   a. disagreement
   b. communication
   c. responsibility

3. **Enforcing** probably means ____.
   a. making sure that rules are obeyed
   b. changing rules occasionally
   c. explaining rules

4. **Opposing** probably means ____.

    a. smart

    b. contrasting

    c. similar

5. **Perceive** probably means ____.

    a. view

    b. enjoy

    c. dislike

C. Choose five words from Activities A and B. Write a sentence using each word. Then take turns reading your sentences aloud to a partner.

1. _____

2. _____

3. _____

4. _____

5. _____

iQ ONLINE   **D.** Go online for more practice with understanding meaning from context.

SPEAKING

At the end of this unit, you are going to give a presentation about how to be an effective leader. As you give the presentation, you will need to check that your audience understands you.

Grammar Gerunds and infinitives

Gerunds (verb + *–ing*) are often used as the subject of a sentence.

☐ **Leading** your team members is a tough job.

Gerunds are also used after prepositions, such as *about*, *of*, *in*, *for*, and *against*, and after certain verbs, such as *consider*, *suggest*, and *recommend*.

☐ Joe thought **about accepting** the promotion.
☐ I **considered voting** for him.

Infinitives (*to* + verb) are often used after the adjective phrase *be* + adjective.

☐ It **is important to respect** your employees.

Infinitives are also used after certain verbs, such as *want*, *decide*, *try*, *hope*, *need*, *expect*, *agree*, and *learn*.

☐ She **hopes to become** a manager one day.

A. Read the sentences. Underline each gerund and infinitive.

1. When Ginny Pitcher needed to hire a director of business development, she turned to her closest friend, Kate Massey.

2. As for the subordinate, he or she needs to understand that the boss can't show any favoritism.

3. Knowing someone will fit in doesn't alleviate other problems.

4. Managing friends isn't always a choice.

5. Gena Cox … suggests saying something like this: "I still want us to be friends."

6. Consider talking to your friend about these problems sooner rather than later.

7. "I didn't jump on it immediately," says Massey. "I thought about taking the job for a while."

B. Complete each sentence with the gerund or infinitive form of the verb in parentheses. Then practice saying the sentences with a partner.

1. Haya expects _____ (finish) business school in June.

2. This book recommends _____ (hire) people you already know.

3. _____ (work) for the government has been a great learning experience.

4. It is difficult _____ (work) while you go to school.

5. Although it took me several months, I finally learned _____ (communicate) effectively with my manager.

6. I suggest _____ (discuss) this with your partner before you make a final decision.

7. We need _____ (discuss) this problem immediately.

8. Jamal was interested in _____ (move) to Hong Kong, but he decided _____ (wait) until next year.

C. Go online for more practice with gerunds and infinitives.

D. Go online for the grammar expansion.

Pronunciation Syllable stress

Every word with more than one **syllable** has a syllable that is **stressed** more than the others. That stressed syllable is longer, and it has a change in pitch.

Listen to the word *negotiate*. Then repeat it.

> negotiate

The second syllable (*-go-*) is stressed. The vowel in this syllable is extra long, and it has a change in pitch.

Listen to the word again and practice saying it, stressing the second syllable.

> negotiate

Every word has its own stress pattern. Using correct word stress will make your speech clearer and easier to understand. When you learn a new word, also take note of the correct stress pattern for that word.

Tip for Success

Many dictionaries show a pronunciation guide for each entry. The pronunciation guide shows the correct syllable stress. Use a dictionary regularly to learn the stress patterns of new words.

A. Listen to the words. Which syllable is stressed? Circle each stressed syllable.

1. (ex)cerpt	5. leadership	9. promotion
2. aspect	6. acknowledge	10. interaction
3. enforce	7. perspective	
4. effective	8. opposing	

B. Listen again. Then practice with a partner. Take turns saying the words.

iQ ONLINE **C.** Go online for more practice with syllable stress.

Speaking Skill | Checking for understanding

When you're giving a presentation or having a conversation, occasionally check that you are clearly communicating your ideas. To check that your listeners understand your main point(s), you can use phrases like these.

Do you know what I mean?	Are you following me?
Does that make sense?	Any questions (so far)?
Do you understand?	

Critical Thinking Tip

Activity B asks you to **summarize** the main points the speaker wants to communicate. When you summarize, you give a shorter version of what you heard or read, including only the main points. Summarizing shows you understand the material.

A. Listen to a manager giving instructions to her staff. Check (✓) the phrases she uses to check for understanding.

☐ Do you know what I mean?   ☐ Are you following me?
☐ Do you know what I'm saying? ☐ Are you with me so far?
☐ Does that make sense?   ☐ Have you got it?
☐ Does everyone understand?   ☐ Got it?

B. Listen again. Then work with a partner. Summarize the main points the manager wants to communicate.

iQ ONLINE **C.** Go online for more practice with checking for understanding.

Unit Assignment | Give a presentation on how to be an effective leader

UNIT OBJECTIVE

In this assignment, you are going to give a short presentation about how to be an effective leader. As you prepare your presentation, think about the Unit Question, "What makes a good leader?" Use information from Listening 1, Listening 2, the unit video, and your work in this unit to support your presentation. Refer to the Self-Assessment checklist on page 24.

CONSIDER THE IDEAS

Read about a paradox, a situation that has two opposite qualities at the same time. In a group, discuss what the author means by a *power paradox*.

The Power Paradox

The best leaders understand the needs and goals of the people they lead. They are careful thinkers who understand the challenges they face. They have the ability to make intelligent choices about how to address those challenges. Great leaders are also communicators. They can explain both problems and solutions to people in a way that everyone can understand.

These abilities are not common, and when we recognize them in someone—in the business world or some other field—we are inspired to say, "That's someone I can trust! That's someone I can follow!" Unfortunately, these abilities also tend to disappear once a person actually takes on a position of leadership.

The British historian Lord Acton once said, "Power tends to corrupt, and absolute power corrupts absolutely." Researchers are now finding scientific support for Acton's claim. Many studies have shown that power can lead people to act without thinking carefully about their decisions. It can also lead people to ignore or misunderstand other people's feelings and desires.

Researchers have created experiments to see how people react when they are given power. The people who were given power over others were more likely to make risky choices, to act aggressively, to speak rudely, and to behave in ways that made others feel scared and uncomfortable. They were also more likely to tease their colleagues.

This is why we call it the *power paradox*. Power is given to people who show an ability to understand, guide, and communicate with others. But, unfortunately, once they become leaders, their power has the potential to make them rude and insensitive. In other words, what people respect and want most from leaders is often what can be damaged when someone has power.

PREPARE AND SPEAK

A. **GATHER IDEAS** Review the information in "The Power Paradox" about how power can affect people. Then think about the information you learned in this unit about people in positions of power. Discuss these questions with a partner.

1. What are some important skills and qualities of a leader?

2. What are negative effects that come from having power?

B. **ORGANIZE IDEAS** Choose two qualities and two problems from Activity A that you think are most important. Place these ideas in the chart. Then suggest ways to develop those qualities and avoid the negative effects.

Important leadership qualities	Ways to develop these qualities
Negative effects of power that leaders can develop	**Ways to avoid these effects**

C. **SPEAK** Present your advice to the class. As you speak, check that your classmates understand the ideas you are trying to communicate. Refer to the Self-Assessment checklist below before you begin.

 Go online for your alternate Unit Assignment.

CHECK AND REFLECT

A. **CHECK** Think about the Unit Assignment as you complete the Self-Assessment checklist.

SELF-ASSESSMENT		
Yes	**No**	
☐	☐	I was able to speak easily about the topic.
☐	☐	My partner, group, and class understood me.
☐	☐	I understood meaning from context.
☐	☐	I used vocabulary from the unit.
☐	☐	I checked for understanding.
☐	☐	I used correct syllable stress.

B. **REFLECT** Go to the Online Dicussion Board to discuss these questions.

1. What is something new you learned in this unit?

2. Look back at the Unit Question—What makes a good leader? Is your answer different now than when you started this unit? If yes, how is it different? Why?

TRACK YOUR SUCCESS

Circle the words you have learned in this unit.

Nouns	Verbs	Adjectives
aspect 🔑 AWL	acknowledge 🔑 AWL	capable 🔑 AWL
contact 🔑 AWL	address 🔑	effective 🔑
criticism 🔑	advance 🔑	ethical AWL
executive 🔑	assess AWL	
expert 🔑 AWL	exemplify	
favoritism	negotiate	
issue 🔑 AWL	outline 🔑	
perspective 🔑 AWL		
potential 🔑 AWL		
staff 🔑		
style 🔑 AWL		
title 🔑		

🔑 Oxford 3000™ words
AWL Academic Word List

Check (✓) the skills you learned. If you need more work on a skill, refer to the page(s) in parentheses.

NOTE TAKING ■	I can use a chart to organize notes about main ideas. (p. 5)
LISTENING ■	I can listen for main ideas. (p. 11)
VOCABULARY ■	I can understand meaning from context. (p. 17)
GRAMMAR ■	I can use gerunds and infinitives. (p. 20)
PRONUNCIATION ■	I can use syllable stress. (p. 21)
SPEAKING ■	I can check for understanding. (p. 22)
UNIT OBJECTIVE ▶▶▶▶ ■	I can gather information and ideas to give a presentation on how to be an effective leader.

UNIT		
2	LISTENING ▶	identifying details
	NOTE TAKING ▶	taking notes using a T-chart
	VOCABULARY ▶	using the dictionary
	GRAMMAR ▶	subjunctive for suggestions
	PRONUNCIATION ▶	unstressed syllables
Behavioral Science	SPEAKING ▶	confirming understanding

UNIT QUESTION

How does appearance affect our success?

A Discuss these questions with your classmates.

1. Think about some successful people. How would you describe each person's appearance?

2. When you are at work or school, is the space around you usually neat or messy? What does a messy desk tell you about the owner's personality?

3. Look at the photo. What does this work space tell you about the person that works here? Would you work in a space like this?

⧩ **B** Listen to *The Q Classroom* online. Then answer these questions.

1. Sophy believes that how we dress affects what people think of us. Do you agree or disagree? Why?

2. Felix argues that not all successful people need to dress well. In addition to athletes, what professionals might have more freedom when it comes to deciding what to wear?

 C Go to the Online Discussion Board to discuss the Unit Question with your classmates.

D What is your first impression of the people in the pictures below? Discuss the questions with a partner.

1. Which person would you most like to work with? Why?

2. How would you describe each person's character?

3. Which person do you think you have the most in common with?

E Look at the behaviors in the chart. Check (✓) if each one would help, hurt, or have no effect on someone's success in the workplace. Compare answers with a partner.

	Help	Hurt	Have no effect
dress like other people in the workplace	☐	☐	☐
dress differently to be noticed	☐	☐	☐
eat with one's co-workers	☐	☐	☐
play sports on the company team	☐	☐	☐
keep one's work space neat	☐	☐	☐
be well-groomed	☐	☐	☐
display one's degrees and professional certificates	☐	☐	☐
have personal pictures at one's desk	☐	☐	☐

LISTENING

LISTENING 1 | A Perfect Mess

UNIT OBJECTIVE ▶▶▶

You are going to listen to a review of a book about mess. The book compares people who are neat to people who aren't. It explores who is more successful. As you listen to the review, gather information and ideas about how appearance affects our success.

PREVIEW THE LISTENING

A. **PREVIEW** Look at the statements below. Check (✓) the statements you agree with.

☐ Messy people are never very organized.

☐ Children should not focus too much on neatness.

☐ Neatness is required in order to work effectively.

☐ It is OK to be a little messy at home.

B. **VOCABULARY** Read aloud these words from Listening 1. Check (✓) the ones you know. Use a dictionary to define any new or unknown words. Then discuss with a partner how the words will relate to the unit.

bias *(n.)*	**moderately** *(adv.)*	**stifle** *(v.)*
chaos *(n.)*	**open-minded** *(adj.)*	**stimulating** *(adj.)*
embrace *(v.)*	**point out** *(phr. v.)*	**stumble upon** *(phr. v.)*
inflexible *(adj.)*	**recognize** *(v.)* 🔑	**turn out** *(phr. v.)*

🔑 Oxford 3000™ words

 C. Go online to listen and practice your pronunciation.

WORK WITH THE LISTENING

◑ **A.** **LISTEN AND TAKE NOTES** Listen to the review and take notes in the chart.

Benefits of being messy	Main ideas and key phrases
At work	
At home	

B. Imagine you were the police chief in Pennsylvania who was fired because of his messy desk. Use your notes to explain why you should get your job back. Write two sentences and share them with a partner.

1. _____

2. _____

C. Read the statements. Write *T* (true) or *F* (false). Then correct the false statements.

____ 1. Moderate messiness seems to be good for people.

____ 2. Messy homes are cold and impersonal.

____ 3. Messy environments are not stimulating enough for children.

____ 4. Messy people tend to be more creative and open-minded.

D. Read the sentences. Then listen again. Circle the answer that best completes each statement.

1. ____ was a very messy but open-minded author.
   a. Albert Einstein
   b. Leon Heppel
   c. Agatha Christie

2. Keeping a house ____ can be bad for a child's health.
   a. too clean
   b. too dirty
   c. too stimulating

3. A messy desk helped ____ two researchers' work.
   a. cause confusion about
   b. show a connection between
   c. find errors in

4. No one at the NAPO conference could answer the question ____.
   a. "Why are people fined at work?"
   b. "What's wrong with being messy?"
   c. "Why is there a bias toward neatness?"

5. Henry Rubins liked his room to be messy because ____.

    a. chaos made him feel comfortable

    b. he had to be neat at work

    c. it made his mother angry

6. A woman in Australia was fined $2,000 because ____.

    a. she had too many papers on her desk

    b. she had too many personal items on her desk

    c. she had a messy desk

E. **Read the sentences about the two examples of messy success stories. Who is each sentence about? Write *LH* (Leon Heppel) or *AC* (Agatha Christie).**

____ 1. This messy person is a researcher at the National Institutes of Health.

____ 2. This messy person compared the information in two different letters.

____ 3. This messy person wrote ideas in disorganized notebooks.

____ 4. This messy person won a Nobel Prize.

____ 5. This messy person wrote very popular novels.

____ 6. This messy person lost important papers in the mess on the desk.

Vocabulary Skill Review

In Unit 1, you learned about understanding meaning from context. Remember to search the context of an unknown word for clues about its meaning. Look beyond the word's phrase to the sentence or even the text as a whole.

F. **VOCABULARY** **Here are some words from Listening 1. Read the sentences. Circle the answer that best matches the meaning of each bold word or phrase.**

1. We hope everyone will **embrace** our new plan for the class trip. We think you will really like the new destination!

    a. be unwilling to accept

    b. accept an idea with enthusiasm

    c. be concerned about

2. I don't want to **stifle** your creativity, but your ideas for the brochure are too complicated. Let's try to make it very simple.

    a. let go of something

    b. prevent something from happening

    c. support something strongly

3. A mother often has a **bias** toward her own children. She sometimes thinks they are better than other children.

    a. hope for

    b. thoughts about

    c. preference for

4. You need to **point out** in your job application why you think you are qualified for the job. It's important that the interviewer understand your skills and experience.

   a. look at something carefully

   b. make something clear

   c. consider someone's ideas

5. The student was **moderately** successful last semester. He didn't fail any classes, but he didn't get excellent grades, either.

   a. not at all

   b. fairly, but not very

   c. extremely

6. I couldn't find my book, and then I happened to **stumble upon** it at my friend's house. It was there the whole time!

   a. find by accident

   b. hit quickly

   c. damage

7. We worked hard all week, but finally we had to **recognize** that we weren't going to finish the project on time.

   a. acknowledge

   b. discourage

   c. ignore

8. The museum was **stimulating**. I was so excited about what I saw that I went back the next day.

   a. expensive

   b. boring

   c. interesting

9. I was worried, but I think the event will **turn out** fine. It looks like we have everything under control.

   a. increase to a new level

   b. change direction quickly

   c. happen with a particular result

10. I am an **open-minded** person. Just because something is different doesn't mean I won't like it.

   a. afraid of trying new things

   b. careless with someone's property

   c. willing to accept new ideas or opinions

11. The chef is very **inflexible**. He always uses the same recipes. He does not like to try new ideas.
    a. unfriendly to others
    b. unsure of the answer
    c. unwilling to change

12. The little boy's room was complete **chaos**. Books, clothes, and games were scattered all over the floor.
    a. a big mess
    b. orderly and neat
    c. well-organized

 **G.** Go online for more practice with the vocabulary.

SAY WHAT YOU THINK

Discuss the questions in a group.

1. How messy are you? Do you agree with the authors of *A Perfect Mess* about the benefits of being a bit messy? Why or why not?

2. How much freedom to be messy should workers have in their work space?

3. When you were a child, were you neat or messy? Have you changed at all as you have gotten older? How?

| Listening Skill | Identifying details |

When you listen to a long presentation or lecture, it's difficult to take notes on everything. It's important to focus on details that support the main ideas you hear. Ask yourself three questions as you listen.

> Is this new information?
> Does this information support the main idea?
> Is this information repeated or rephrased?

If you answer yes to any of these questions, the detail may be important to remember.

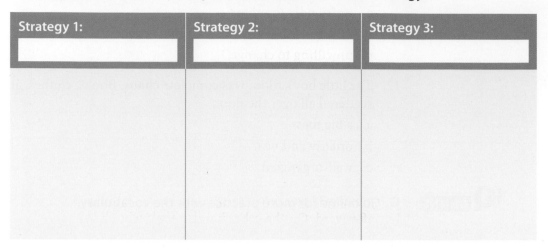

A. Listen to a short lecture about three strategies for being more organized. Complete the chart with important details about each strategy.

Tip for Success

Use abbreviations and symbols when you take notes. This will make it easier to take notes quickly. Then review your notes to make sure your ideas are clear.

Strategy 1:	Strategy 2:	Strategy 3:

B. Work with a partner. Compare your notes. Ask each other the following questions. If you answer *no* to a question, revise your notes.

1. Does this information support the main idea?

2. Is this information repeated or rephrased?

 C. Go online for more practice with identifying details.

Note-taking Skill Taking notes using a T-chart

A T-chart is a useful way to take notes about two contrasting topics. When you are reading a text or listening to something about two sides of an issue or two different ideas, make a T-chart by drawing a "T." Write the two topics at the top and make notes under each topic. In some cases, you can write an idea about a topic directly across from the related idea on the other side. Look at the example T-chart below listing some arguments for and against being messy.

Arguments for being messy	Arguments against being messy
• Things can be easier to find because they're right out in the open. • Being messy can help people connect ideas in new ways	• It's easier to lose or misplace the things we need. • Being messy can set a bad example for children.

A. Read and listen to the presentation about the benefits of a happy appearance. Complete the notes in the T-chart.

Sure, we all look better when we smile, but can our facial expressions really cause us to succeed or fail? Many scientists believe that smiling can lead to more success in life, whereas frowning can lead to more problems. Some researchers discovered that people who smiled in school pictures were more likely to have longer, happier marriages in the future than those who did not. In contrast, people who didn't smile in their class photos tended to get divorced more often. Also, people who smiled in job interviews were more likely to get the jobs than candidates who didn't smile. Smiling also reduces stress, some scientists say. In fact, in one study, smiling while doing a stressful job helped workers' brains and bodies recover from the stress more quickly afterward. On the other hand, people who didn't smile had faster heartbeats long after they finished the stressful job. Maybe this is why smiling can even cause people to live longer. One research study discovered that if baseball players were smiling on their cards, they lived almost seven years longer than players who weren't smiling. So, remember to smile!

Happy facial expressions	Serious facial expressions
• longer, happier marriages	• _____
• more likely to get job after an interview	• _____
• _____	• more stress
• _____	• faster heartbeats after stressful job was finished

 B. Go online for more practice taking notes using a T-chart.

LISTENING 2 | The Changing Business Dress Code

You are going to listen to a radio talk show in which two experts discuss dressing for work. As you listen to the talk show, gather information and ideas about how appearance affects our success.

PREVIEW THE LISTENING

A. **PREVIEW** Work with a partner. Discuss these questions.

1. How does your appearance at work affect how you feel?

2. Does it affect the way you do your job? Why or why not?

B. **VOCABULARY** Read aloud these words from Listening 2. Check (✓) the ones you know. Use a dictionary to define any new or unknown words. Then discuss with a partner how the words will relate to the unit.

anecdote (n.)	cautious (adj.)	enthusiasm (n.) 🔑	norm (n.)
appropriate (adj.) 🔑	conduct (v.) 🔑	investor (n.)	reward (n.) 🔑
associate (v.) 🔑	cycle (n.) 🔑	morale (n.)	trend (n.) 🔑

🔑 Oxford 3000™ words

 **C.** Go online to listen and practice your pronunciation.

WORK WITH THE LISTENING

A. **LISTEN AND TAKE NOTES** Listen to the radio talk show and take notes in the T-chart.

Positive effects of casual business clothing	Negative effects of casual business clothing

B. Use your notes to help you answer the questions. Compare your answers with a partner.

1. Why did executives think casual dress would be a good idea when it started?

2. Why are investors more cautious about casually dressed business executives?

3. What is casual or sloppy dress sometimes associated with?

4. What type of clothing do many young people now wear at work?

C. Read the questions. Then listen again. Circle the correct answers.

1. According to Andrew Park, what is the current trend for business dress codes?
   a. Casual dress is becoming the norm.
   b. More formal dress is becoming popular again.
   c. Employees can dress however they want to dress.

2. How has casual dress affected some businesses?
   a. It has had a negative effect on the way clients see them.
   b. It has had a negative effect on the employees' morale.
   c. It has had a negative effect on CEOs' productivity.

3. What does Andrew Park say about fashion in the workplace?
   a. Older people will always dress more formally than young people.
   b. Fashion trends go in cycles, from formal to informal and back again.
   c. CEOs dress more formally than their employees.

4. According to the speakers, what does the way we dress tell other people?
   a. It tells people how fashion moves in cycles.
   b. It tells people where we work.
   c. It tells people who we are.

D. Read the excerpt from the radio talk show. Complete Andrew Park's paragraph with the correct words. Then listen and check your answers.

accepted	cycles	lifestyle	natural	uniform
connected	formally	managers	professional	workplace

But fashion trends always go in _____. In the '50s
                                      1

and early '60s, the business _____ for men in the
                              2

United States was a suit and tie. Working women wore a suit or a dress and jacket. The look was _____. Then in the '60s and

'70s, young people gave up that look. They _____
_____ **4**

the suit and tie with older people and older ways of thinking. They

wanted a more _____, back-to-basics kind of
_____ **5**

_____. The children who grew up during the
_____ **6**

'60s and '70s became _____ in the '80s and '90s.
_____ **7**

They were the ones who _____ casual dress
_____ **8**

in the _____. When one generation dresses
_____ **9**

_____, the next wants to be casual, and so on. That's
_____ **10**

the way fashion works.

E. Imagine your school wanted to start a Formal Friday when all students would have to dress in formal business clothing. Do you think this would be a good idea? Discuss your ideas with a partner.

Tip for Success

To really learn a word, most people need to see and use the word many times. Making flashcards with new words and studying them often is a good way to review the words.

F. **VOCABULARY** Here are some words from Listening 2. Complete each sentence with the correct word.

anecdote (n.)	cautious (adj.)	enthusiasm (n.)	norm (n.)
appropriate (adj.)	conduct (v.)	investor (n.)	reward (n.)
associate (v.)	cycle (n.)	morale (n.)	trend (n.)

1. Andrew knew first impressions are important. He thought about what would be most _____ to wear for his job interview.

2. When the team lost its tenth game in a row, _____ among the players and the fans was very low. Everyone seemed sad.

3. In the past, many people worked for large companies. Now there is a _____ toward more people working for small businesses.

4. The employees at our office usually work long hours. I'd say the _____ is about 60 hours a week.

5. Ming gave us a lot of money to open our new store. She is our most important _____.

6. The employees worked hard to finish the project on time. As a _____, their boss gave them an extra day off.

7. Clothing style goes in a _____. Something becomes popular. Then it's out of style, and then it's in style again.

8. My grandfather once told me a(n) _____ about what he did when he was a little boy.

9. I always _____ that book with my senior year in high school. I remember reading it in class.

10. The government decided to _____ a study on the effects of caffeine.

11. My uncle enjoyed playing soccer his whole life. He never lost his _____ for it.

12. The woman was _____ as she walked down the icy stairs. She was concerned that she might fall and get hurt.

 **G.** Go online for more practice with the vocabulary.

H. Go online to listen to *Appearances Matter in the Animal World* and check your comprehension.

 SAY WHAT YOU THINK

A. Discuss the questions in a group.

1. If you were a manager, how would appearance affect an employee's chance for promotion?

2. Have you ever worn a uniform for work or school? Did you like it? What are some advantages and disadvantages of wearing a uniform?

B. Go online to watch a video about messy desks. Then check your comprehension.

clutter *(n.)* things that make a place messy

efficiency *(n.)* the ability to work well without wasting time or energy

filthy *(adj.)* dirty

tidy *(adj.)* arranged in good order; neat

C. Think about the unit video, Listening 1, and Listening 2 as you discuss the questions.

1. How much do a person's clothing and organizational skills affect your first impression of him or her?

2. Think about a time that you judged someone based on how he or she looked or organized things. Was your first impression right or wrong? Why?

Vocabulary Skill   Using the dictionary

When you look a word up in the dictionary, there are often several different **definitions** given. You must consider the context of the word to choose the correct definition.

Decide what part of speech the word is in that context—for example, a *noun* or a *verb*. When you look up the word, you can then quickly eliminate a form or use of the word not appropriate to the context.

> In many places, casual Fridays are starting to **fade**, and there's a move toward "dress-up" or "formal" Thursdays or Mondays.

fade /feɪd/ *verb* **1** [I, T] to become, or to make something become, paler or less bright: *The curtains had faded in the sun.* ♦ **~ from sth** *All color had faded from her face.* ♦ **~ sth** *The sun had faded the curtains.* ♦ *He was wearing faded blue jeans.* **2** [I] to disappear gradually: *Her smile faded.* ♦ **~ away** *Hopes of reaching an agreement seem to be fading away.* ♦ *The laughter faded away.* ♦ **~ to/into sth** *His voice faded to a whisper* (= gradually became quieter). ♦ *All other issues fade into insignificance compared with the struggle for survival.* **3** [I] if a sports player, team, etc. **fades**, they stop playing or performing as well as they did before: *Black faded on the final bend.* **IDM** **see** WOODWORK

Read all of the definitions before you make the choice. By thinking about the context of the report, you can conclude that the first definition of *fade* is not correct in this context.

All dictionary entries are from the *Oxford Advanced American Dictionary for learners of English* © Oxford University Press 2011.

A. Read each sentence. Then circle the correct definition of each bold word.

1. Employees were allowed to **ditch** their suits and ties and formal skirts.

> **ditch** /dɪtʃ/ noun, verb
> • **noun** a long channel dug at the side of a field or road, to hold or take away water
> • **verb 1** [T] ~ **sth/sb** (informal) to get rid of something or someone because you no longer want or need it/them: *The new road building program has been ditched.* **2** [T, I] ~ **(sth)** if a pilot **ditches** an aircraft, or if it **ditches**, it lands in the ocean in an emergency **3** [T] ~ **school** (informal) to stay away from school without permission

2. A very neat home can be impersonal and **cold**. A messy house can show your personality.

> **cold** 🔑 /koʊld/ adj., noun, adv.
> • **adj.** (cold·er, cold·est)
> > **LOW TEMPERATURE 1** having a lower than usual temperature; having a temperature lower than the human body: *I'm cold. Turn the heat up.* ♦ *to feel/look cold* ♦ *cold hands and feet* ♦ *a cold room/house* ♦ *Isn't it cold today?* ♦ *It's freezing cold.* ♦ *to get/turn colder* ♦ *bitterly cold weather* ♦ *the coldest May on record*
> > **FOOD/DRINKS 2** not heated; cooled after being cooked: *a cold drink* ♦ *Hot and cold food is available in the cafeteria.* ♦ *cold chicken for lunch*
> > **UNFRIENDLY 3** (of a person) without emotion; unfriendly: *to give someone a cold look/stare/welcome* ♦ *Her manner was cold and distant.* ♦ *He was staring at her with cold eyes.*

B. Read each sentence. Then look up the definition of the bold word. Write the correct definition for the context of each bold word.

1. I found out how **deep** the world's bias toward neatness and order is.

_____

2. The woman received a **fine** of more than two thousand dollars at work.

_____

3. They're looking for a **sign** that people are professional.

_____

4. I have been messy since I was old enough to **dress** myself.

_____

iQ ONLINE **C.** Go online for more practice with using the dictionary.

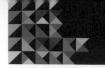

SPEAKING

At the end of this unit, you are going to role-play a conversation offering advice to help someone become better organized. You will need to be able to confirm understanding during the conversation.

Grammar	Subjunctive for suggestions

The **subjunctive** is the simple or base form of a verb—for example, "go" or "try."

You can use the subjunctive to talk about events that you want to happen or hope will happen. You also use it to make a strong suggestion about something that you think should happen.

This structure is formed in two ways.

1. **suggesting verb + indirect object (IO) + base form of verb**
2. **suggesting expression + indirect object (IO) + base form of verb**

His boss <u>recommended</u> that <u>he</u> <u>wear</u> a suit for the meeting tomorrow.
        suggesting verb   IO base form of verb

<u>It is important that</u> <u>employees</u> <u>be</u> professional at all times.
  suggesting expression   IO   base form of verb

The subjunctive doesn't change form according to the person.

> I recommend that **you work** harder.
> I recommend that **he work** harder.
> I recommend that **they work** harder.

It also doesn't change tense when the main verb is in the past tense.

> I recommend**ed** that he **work** harder.

To make a negative suggestion, insert *not* between the indirect object and the base form of the verb.

> It's essential that employees **not** show up late for meetings.

Certain verbs and certain expressions are often used with the subjunctive to make suggestions and recommendations. The word *that* is always optional.

Some verbs followed by the subjunctive	Some expressions followed by the subjunctive
to advise (that)	It's best (that)
to ask (that)	It's desirable (that)
to desire (that)	It's essential (that)
to insist (that)	It's important (that)
to recommend (that)	It's recommended (that)
to request (that)	It's a good idea (that)
to suggest (that)	It's preferred (that)

A. Rewrite the sentences. Use the subjunctive.

1. Customers expect sales reps to dress more formally.

   Customers request that sales reps _____.

2. Employees should try to avoid looking sloppy at work.

   It is recommended that employees _____.

3. When CEOs pose for a work-related picture, they should not wear jeans and sandals.

   When CEOs pose for a work-related picture, it's important that they

   _____.

4. Some executives want their employees to ditch their casual clothes.

   Some executives advise that employees _____.

5. Some experts say that managers should offer a "dress-up Monday" option.

   Some experts suggest that managers _____.

6. I think that people dressing more formally at work is a good idea.

   It's a good idea that people _____.

B. Look at the pictures. Write advice for each person on how to dress. Use the subjunctive. Then share your advice with a partner.

Picture A

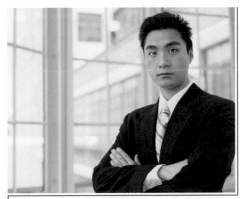
Picture B

Picture A: This man just started working in a very formal office.

1. _____

2. _____

Picture B: This man is going to start working in a casual office.

1. _____

2. _____

 **C.** Go online for more practice with the subjunctive.

D. Go online for the grammar expansion.

Pronunciation   Unstressed syllables

Vowels in stressed syllables are long and clear. In contrast, vowels in unstressed syllables are often reduced to a short sound called a *schwa* (/ə/). It is the most common vowel sound.

Listen to this word.

appearances

The stressed syllable is the second syllable: *ap-PEAR-an-ces*. The vowel sounds in the unstressed syllables are pronounced /ə/.

/əpɪr•ən•səz/

To make the /ə/ sound, drop your jaw a little and relax your tongue. It is a very short, "lazy" sound.

A. Listen to the words. Which syllables are unstressed? Cross out the unstressed syllables in each word.

Tip for Success

Some online dictionaries have word pronunciations that you can click on. This is a good way to quickly learn the unstressed syllables in new words.

1. pleasure   5. business

2. forgotten   6. allow

3. successful   7. cautious

4. habit   8. professional

B. Listen again. Repeat the words. Focus on the unstressed syllables.

 C. Go online for more practice with unstressed syllables.

Speaking Skill | Confirming understanding

Sometimes you might think that you understand what someone is saying, but you are not exactly sure. These are ways you can check your understanding.

Ask a question that signals your need to confirm your understanding.

> Do you mean that . . . ?
> Excuse me, are you saying . . . ?
> Does that mean . . . ?

Restate what the speaker said in your own words.

> If I understand you, . . .
> (So) you're saying that . . .

After the speaker responds, let the speaker know that you now understand the information. You can do this by using phrases like *thanks*, *OK*, *right*, *I see*, or *got it*.

Critical Thinking **Tip**

In the Speaking Skill activities, you practice restating what a speaker has said. When you **restate** information, you will understand and remember it better.

A. Listen to the conversations. Complete the conversations using expressions from the Speaking Skill box. Then practice the conversations with a partner.

1. **A:** Did you hear that starting next month there won't be a "casual Friday" anymore?

   B: What? _____ they are getting rid of casual Friday completely?

   A: Yes, the email said no more casual Fridays.

   B: Oh.

2. **A:** More and more customers are looking for a sign of professionalism.

   B: _____ they prefer less casual dress?

   A: Yeah, that's right.

   B: _____.

3. **A:** If my desk is too organized, I can't be creative.

   B: _____, you need to be messy to work well?

   A: Yeah, I need a little mess.

   B: _____.

4. A: Most people can't get organized all at once.

   B: _____ it's better to work on it step by step?

   A: Yes, it does.

   B: _____.

Tip for Success

Confirming understanding is a great way to participate actively in a conversation. It shows others you are listening and interested.

B. Work in a group. Discuss the questions. Use questions and phrases from the Speaking Skill box to confirm your understanding.

1. What connection is there between appearance and quality of work? Do you think that when people look sloppy, they are less careful at work?

2. Do people's appearance and the condition of their workspace matter if they can get the job done?

3. Do you think that schools should teach students how to be organized?

iQ ONLINE **C.** Go online for more practice with confirming understanding.

Unit Assignment Role-play

UNIT OBJECTIVE ▶▶▶▶ In this assignment, you are going to role-play a conversation offering advice to help someone become better organized. As you prepare your role-play, think about the Unit Question, "How does appearance affect our success?" Use information from Listening 1, Listening 2, the unit video, and your work in this unit to support your role-play. Refer to the Self-Assessment checklist on page 48.

CONSIDER THE IDEAS

In a group, make a list of situations that can create a mess at school or at work (for example, too many piles of paper, not enough storage space, too many personal belongings, etc.). Discuss ways to make the situations better.

_____

_____

_____

_____

_____

PREPARE AND SPEAK

A. **GATHER IDEAS** Imagine you are in a business to help clients get organized. Read about a new client. Take notes on his situation.

Name: Dan Howard

Occupation: Sales representative

The Situation: A few years ago, I had the best sales record in my department. My customers respected me, and they were loyal to me. In the past couple of years, however, my sales have dropped. I was doing OK until my manager moved me into a smaller office. There is less storage space for my paperwork. Now I can't find anything. I have piles of customers' papers everywhere. I even lost my phone last week. My old customers don't ask for my help anymore. The few new customers I have don't seem to trust me. I can't blame them. I can't find anything they need. My sales are now the worst in my department. I need help!

Problems	Details

B. **ORGANIZE IDEAS** What advice would you offer to help Dan Howard? Write notes about three pieces of advice you would give him. Give details and examples to support your advice.

Advice to improve the situation	Details and examples
1.	
2.	
3.	

C. SPEAK Work with your partner. Role-play a conversation in which one of you gives advice and one of you is Dan Howard. The person giving advice should use the subjunctive when appropriate, and the person playing Dan Howard should confirm understanding. Present the role-play to the class. Refer to the Self-Assessment checklist below before you begin.

 Go online for your alternate Unit Assignment.

CHECK AND REFLECT

A. CHECK Think about the Unit Assignment as you complete the Self-Assessment checklist.

SELF-ASSESSMENT		
Yes	No	
☐	☐	I was able to speak easily about the topic.
☐	☐	My partner, group, and class understood me.
☐	☐	I used a T-chart to take notes.
☐	☐	I used the subjunctive.
☐	☐	I used vocabulary from the unit.
☐	☐	I confirmed understanding.
☐	☐	I pronounced unstressed syllables correctly.

 B. REFLECT Go to the Online Discussion Board to discuss these questions.

1. What is something new you learned in this unit?

2. Look back at the Unit Question—How does appearance affect our success? Is your answer different now than when you started this unit? If yes, how is it different? Why?

TRACK YOUR SUCCESS

Circle the words you have learned in this unit.

Nouns	Verbs	Adjectives
anecdote	associate 🔑	appropriate 🔑 AWL
bias AWL	conduct 🔑 AWL	cautious
chaos	embrace	inflexible AWL
cycle 🔑 AWL	recognize 🔑	open-minded
enthusiasm 🔑	stifle	stimulating
investor AWL	**Phrasal Verbs**	**Adverb**
morale	point out	moderately
norm AWL	stumble upon	
reward 🔑	turn out	
trend 🔑 AWL		

🔑 Oxford 3000™ words

AWL Academic Word List

Check (✓) the skills you learned. If you need more work on a skill, refer to the page(s) in parentheses.

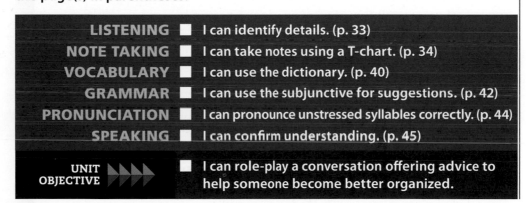

LISTENING	☐	I can identify details. (p. 33)
NOTE TAKING	☐	I can take notes using a T-chart. (p. 34)
VOCABULARY	☐	I can use the dictionary. (p. 40)
GRAMMAR	☐	I can use the subjunctive for suggestions. (p. 42)
PRONUNCIATION	☐	I can pronounce unstressed syllables correctly. (p. 44)
SPEAKING	☐	I can confirm understanding. (p. 45)
UNIT OBJECTIVE ▶▶▶▶	☐	I can role-play a conversation offering advice to help someone become better organized.

UNIT 3

Developmental Psychology

NOTE TAKING	▶	taking notes using key words and phrases
LISTENING	▶	making predictions
VOCABULARY	▶	using the dictionary
GRAMMAR	▶	phrasal verbs
PRONUNCIATION	▶	sentence stress
SPEAKING	▶	giving a presentation

UNIT QUESTION

When does a child become an adult?

A Discuss these questions with your classmates.

1. In your opinion, at what age does a person become an adult? Why?
2. What important events or experiences can make you feel more like an adult?
3. Look at the photo. What is the woman doing? How does this event make her an adult?

B Listen to *The Q Classroom* online. Then answer these questions.

1. What events and experiences do Felix and Sophy give as examples of adult behavior? Do you agree with them?
2. Marcus mentions that you become an adult when your body has grown and your mind has developed. Do you think that becoming an adult is more physiological and biological than anything else?

iQ ONLINE **C Go to the Online Discussion Board to discuss the Unit Question with your classmates.**

UNIT
OBJECTIVE

Listen to a phone conversation and a lecture and gather information and ideas to present a personal story.

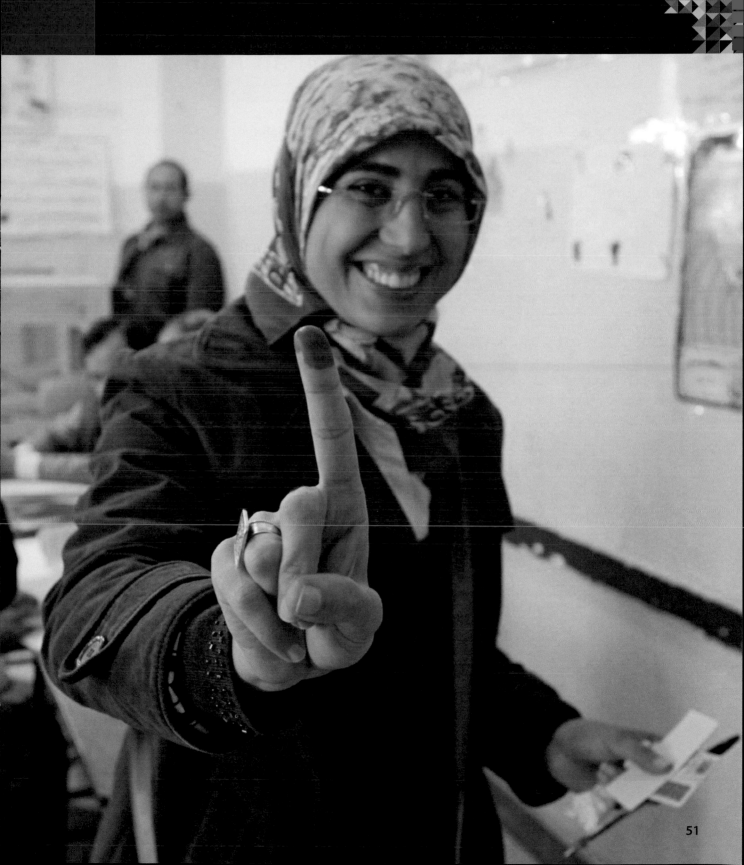

D Which experiences make someone an adult? Check (✓) your top three choices. Work with a partner to compare ideas.

What Makes You an Adult?

- ☐ getting a job
- ☐ finishing high school
- ☐ turning a certain age
- ☐ moving into your own home
- ☐ getting married
- ☐ finishing college
- ☐ making your own big decisions
- ☐ paying all your own expenses
- ☐ traveling without your parents
- ☐ having children
- ☐ other: _____

E Read the proverbs. Do you agree or disagree with them? Why? Discuss your opinions with a partner.

1. Everyone is the age of their heart. (Guatemalan proverb)

2. Only three things in life are certain: birth, death, and change. (Arabic proverb)

3. A child's life is like a piece of paper on which every passerby leaves a mark. (Chinese proverb)

4. We start as fools and become wise through experience. (African proverb)

5. What is learned in youth is carved in stone. (Arabic proverb)

Note-taking Skill | Taking notes using key words and phrases

Trying to write down every word as you listen to a lecture or a presentation is an impossible task. Speakers talk too quickly, repeat themselves, and say things that are not essential to their message. When you listen and take notes, quickly decide which words are important and which words aren't. Write the key words and phrases in your notes.

Here are some tips to help you identify key words and phrases:

- They are directly connected to the topic.
- They communicate the main idea and important supporting details.
- They are usually repeated or rephrased.
- They may be specific names, dates, places, or events.

Do not try to write complete sentences in your notes. Key words and phrases are all you need to help you summarize what you heard.

A. Listen to the presentation about two ceremonies that celebrate becoming an adult. Check (✓) the key words and phrases. Compare your answers with a partner and explain why you have chosen them.

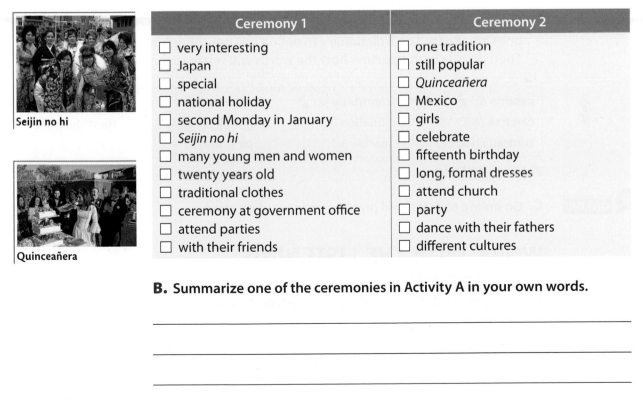

Seijin no hi

Quinceañera

Ceremony 1	Ceremony 2
☐ very interesting	☐ one tradition
☐ Japan	☐ still popular
☐ special	☐ *Quinceañera*
☐ national holiday	☐ Mexico
☐ second Monday in January	☐ girls
☐ *Seijin no hi*	☐ celebrate
☐ many young men and women	☐ fifteenth birthday
☐ twenty years old	☐ long, formal dresses
☐ traditional clothes	☐ attend church
☐ ceremony at government office	☐ party
☐ attend parties	☐ dance with their fathers
☐ with their friends	☐ different cultures

B. Summarize one of the ceremonies in Activity A in your own words.

_____

_____

_____

 C. Go online for more practice taking notes using key words and phrases.

LISTENING

LISTENING 1 | Making the Right Decision

You are going to listen to a phone conversation about an important decision someone makes. As you listen to the conversation, gather information and ideas about when a child becomes an adult.

PREVIEW THE LISTENING

A. **PREVIEW** Before you listen to the conversation, answer these questions. Discuss your ideas with a partner.

1. Sometimes being an adult means doing something you *should* do rather than something you *want* to do. These difficult decisions are sometimes called sacrifices. What are two sacrifices someone might make that demonstrate that he or she has grown up?

2. What sacrifices have you had to make in your life? Have your parents or guardians had to make any sacrifices for you?

B. **VOCABULARY** Read aloud these words from Listening 1. Check (✓) the ones you know. Use a dictionary to define any new or unknown words. Then discuss with a partner how the words will relate to the unit.

assume *(v.)* 🔑	contribute *(v.)* 🔑	milestone *(n.)*	run *(v.)* 🔑
carefree *(adj.)*	initiation *(n.)*	morally *(adv.)* 🔑	transition *(v.)* 🔑
contradiction *(n.)*	marker *(n.)*	pinpoint *(v.)*	

🔑 Oxford 3000™ words

 C. Go online to listen and practice your pronunciation.

WORK WITH THE LISTENING

A. **LISTEN AND TAKE NOTES** Complete the chart with the main points of Neils's story. Write down only the important words. Compare your notes with a partner.

The situation	The problem	The solution

B. Read these statements. Write *T* (true) or *F* (false). Then correct the false statements.

____ 1. Neils was spending a lot of his free time managing the football team at his school.

____ 2. Neils didn't really enjoy his duties as team manager.

____ 3. Because of his role as the football team leader, he didn't have enough time to study as much as he needed to.

____ 4. Neils's parents insisted that he quit the football team.

____ 5. Neils thinks that becoming an adult will mean he has total freedom.

C. Read the questions. Then listen again. Circle the correct answers.

1. What does Neils's grandmother mean when she says that this time is important to his future?
   a. Neils needs to make a big decision right now.
   b. What Neils does now will affect his future.
   c. She is sure that Neils will pass his exams.

2. How has the football team done under Neils's leadership?
   a. They have improved.
   b. They have stayed the same.
   c. They have gotten worse.

3. When did Neils realize that he needed to make a change?
   a. after the team lost a game
   b. after he fell asleep one night
   c. after he failed an important exam

4. Why did Neils quit as the manager of the football team?
   a. He thought he would not be a good example for the boys if he failed his classes.
   b. His grandmother told him to.
   c. He was too tired to continue as the manager.

5. Why is his grandmother so proud of him?
   a. He won a big football game.
   b. He made a difficult decision on his own.
   c. He passed an important exam.

D. Read the comments about Neils's experience. Match each quote with the speaker who probably said it. Compare your answers with a partner. Then come up with one more quote for each speaker.

a. Neils's father	c. Neils's teacher	e. the coach of Neils's team
b. Neils's best friend	d. a player on Neils's team	

____ 1.   We really miss Neils. He was a great team manager because he pushed us to play hard, but he was still a lot of fun.

_____

____ 2.   Neils did the right thing when he quit the team. He is more focused in class, and his test scores have already improved a lot.

_____

____ 3.   The team won't be the same without Neils. His leadership helped our team become very successful, and the boys on the team respected him.

_____

____ 4.   I still don't get to hang out with Neils as much as I want, but he's been less stressed since he quit the football team.

_____

____ 5.   I am really proud of Neils. He made a smart, mature decision and learned a valuable lesson.

_____

Vocabulary Skill Review

In Unit 2, you learned about how different definitions for a word are appropriate in different contexts. Remember to read all of the dictionary definitions carefully when you are looking up a new word. Think about the context of the unit and the topic of the listening to help you identify the correct definition.

E. **VOCABULARY** Here are some words from Listening 1. Complete each sentence with the correct word.

assume *(v.)*	contribute *(v.)*	milestone *(n.)*	run *(v.)*
carefree *(adj.)*	initiation *(n.)*	morally *(adv.)*	transition *(v.)*
contradiction *(n.)*	marker *(n.)*	pinpoint *(v.)*	

1. The _____ into the students' club was a ceremony involving the new members and the old members.

2. If you want to speak to the managers, please talk to Sultan and Mosaad.

   They _____ the department.

3. Some people say an important _____ of maturity is the ability to balance your emotions. It tells others that you are reasonable.

4. My sixteen-year-old son says he wants to be treated like an adult, but then he acts like a child. There's a _____ between what he says and what he does.

5. Most people consider stealing to be _____ wrong. It is not within the social standards for most societies.

6. Did his good attitude _____ to his success?

7. If I don't come to the door when you knock, you can _____ that I'm not home.

8. I like to go on vacation and be _____. It's nice not to have to deal with problems at work for a while.

9. Graduating, buying a home, and getting married were all big _____ in my life.

10. It can be difficult to _____ from one job to another, but the change might be good for your career.

11. I can't _____ the day I started to like cabbage, but I think it was when I was twelve.

 F. Go online for more practice with the vocabulary.

SAY WHAT YOU THINK

Discuss the questions in a group.

1. The United Nations Convention on the Rights of the Child says that anyone under the age of 18 is a child. Do you agree or disagree? Why?

2. Do you think that there should be a formal event to mark adulthood? Why or why not?

3. Neils's grandmother says his decision to quit the team was a milestone in his development. Have you ever had a similar experience that helped you to grow up? What happened?

Predictions are guesses you make based only on the information that is available. For example, you may know the title of a lecture. You can use the title to predict the topic and the ideas it might cover.

Your predictions are also based on what you already know about a topic. Background information from articles you have read, from electronic media, and from previous experiences all help prepare you to understand new information, and to predict what you are likely to hear next.

One way to make predictions is to write down the topic. Then take brief notes on the ideas and vocabulary you already know that are associated with that topic. This prepares you for the information that you will hear, so you don't have to work quite as hard to understand it.

A. Read the lecture titles. Predict the topic of the lecture and the main ideas it might cover. Write brief notes about what you already know about the topic and five words you might expect to hear.

1. Trends in World Architecture (*Architecture Appreciation Lecture*)

   What I know about this topic: _____

   _____

   _____

   Five words I might hear: _____

   _____

2. Global Warming (*Environmental Studies*)

   What I know about this topic: _____

   _____

   _____

   Five words I might hear: _____

   _____

3. Technology in Schools (*Media Studies*)

What I know about this topic: _____

_____

_____

Five words I might hear: _____

_____

B. Read the questions. Then listen to the excerpts. Circle the correct answers.

Excerpt 1

Which of the following is most likely to be discussed in the lecture?

a. what to do when you want a promotion

b. how to explain your side of an argument

c. what kinds of jobs are right for you

Excerpt 2

What is Adam most likely to suggest?

a. Don't take the online class that I took.

b. You should focus on your job.

c. Schedule some time every night just for homework.

Excerpt 3

What is Tara most likely to say next?

a. "You're going to have a wonderful time."

b. "You still owe me some money."

c. "You were never very nice to me."

Excerpt 4

How will the employees most likely feel when they hear the news?

a. worried

b. confused

c. excited

I have some important news.

 C. Go online for more practice making predictions.

LISTENING 2 | Growing Up Quickly

You are going to listen to a lecture about children who have to act like parents. As you listen to the lecture, gather information and ideas about when a child becomes an adult.

PREVIEW THE LISTENING

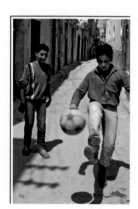

A. **PREVIEW** Children with adult responsibilities might feel many emotions. Circle four emotions these children might feel because of their responsibilities. Discuss your answers with a partner.

embarrassment	frustration	jealousy	pride	sadness
fear	happiness	love	regret	satisfaction

B. **VOCABULARY** Read aloud these words from Listening 2. Check (✓) the ones you know. Use a dictionary to define any new or unknown words. Then discuss with a partner how the words will relate to the unit.

barrier (n.) 🔑	**frustration** (n.)	**isolation** (n.)	**satisfaction** (n.) 🔑
burden (n.)	**guidance** (n.)	**resent** (v.)	**sibling** (n.)
confusion (n.) 🔑	**in charge of** (phr.)	**reverse** (v.) 🔑	

🔑 Oxford 3000™ words

 C. Go online to listen and practice your pronunciation.

WORK WITH THE LISTENING

A. **LISTEN AND TAKE NOTES** Listen to the lecture and complete the notes in the chart. Write only the words that communicate information. Do not try to write every word.

Children acting like adults	Key words and phrases
Reasons some children take on adult responsibilities	younger siblings _____ _____ _____
Examples of parentification	_____ _____ go to parent-teacher meeting
Examples of role reversal	cook for parents _____ take care of parents
Emotions	_____ embarrassment _____ resentment _____

B. Use your notes to summarize the difference between parentification and role reversal. Complete the sentences.

1. Parentification happens when children _____.

2. Role reversal happens when children _____.

C. Listen to the lecture again. Check (✓) the main ideas the lecturer presents.

☐ Too much responsibility can be a burden on children.
☐ Many children have sick family members.
☐ Children often have to take on the role of parent to care for siblings.
☐ Some children even reverse roles with their own parents.
☐ Parents have to provide guidance for their children.
☐ Responsibilities can be barriers and cause frustration.
☐ Many of these children become teachers and counselors.
☐ Many children get satisfaction from helping others.

D. Read the statements. Write *T* (true) or *F* (false). Then correct the false statements.

_____ 1. An older sibling gave Bill some adult responsibilities.

_____ 2. *Parentification* is when children take on the duties of parents.

_____ 3. In a reversed role, the parents make the important decisions.

_____ 4. The effect on a child depends on a child's personality and situation.

_____ 5. Parentified children rarely feel confusion or isolation.

_____ 6. Children usually experience fewer negative effects if they take on responsibilities at a younger age.

_____ 7. Kids with adult responsibilities often care more about others.

_____ 8. Many people in helping professions grew up having some adult responsibilities.

E. Read some examples of children taking on adult responsibilities. Do you think they are examples of *parentification* or role reversal? Write *P* (parentification) and *R* (role reversal). Compare answers with a partner.

_____ 1. A boy helps his younger brother get ready for bed.

_____ 2. A girl is in charge of giving medicine to her father because he is sick in bed.

_____ 3. A girl translates important mail from her brother's school for her mother.

_____ 4. A boy works after school and buys food for his siblings.

_____ 5. A girl helps her younger sister with her homework.

_____ 6. A boy helps his father brush his teeth and wash in the morning.

siblings

F. **VOCABULARY** Here are some words from Listening 2. Read the sentences. Then write each bold word next to the correct definition.

1. My youngest **sibling** is six years younger than I am. We still call him the "baby" of the family.

2. Taking care of my husband's elderly parents is a **burden** but also an honor. It is a lot of work, but I am happy to do it.

3. Max is **in charge of** the entire store. If anyone has a question or complaint, they go to his office.

4. I used to think children should participate in a lot of planned activities, but I **reversed** my opinion. Now I think they should be free to do what they want most of the time.

5. Parents and teachers should provide **guidance** to children to help them with difficult problems.

6. We used to live on a farm far away from any town. I didn't like the **isolation**, but it was very peaceful.

7. There was some **confusion** about what was going to happen. Danielle thought I was going to the beach, and I thought she was going to the beach. Neither of us was right!

8. I **resent** Lawrence for always being late. I think it's disrespectful.

9. When the tree fell, it became a **barrier** in the road and we couldn't drive around it.

10. I felt a lot of **frustration** with my study partner. I knew we could finish our project on time if I helped him with his part, but he insisted on doing it all himself.

11. I like many things about my career, but nothing beats the **satisfaction** of a job well done.

a. _____ (*phr.*) in control of something or someone

b. _____ (*n.*) a responsibility that causes difficulty or hard work

c. _____ (*n.*) a feeling of anger or disappointment

d. _____ (*n.*) the state of being uncertain or not clear

e. _____ (*n.*) a brother or sister

f. _____ (*v.*) to change something to the opposite

g. _____ (*v.*) to feel angry about something because you feel it is unfair

h. _____ (*n.*) a feeling of pleasure when you get something you wanted

i. _____ (*n.*) the state of being separate from other people or being alone

j. _____ (*n.*) a thing or situation that makes something difficult or impossible

k. _____ (*n.*) help or advice

G. Go online for more practice with the vocabulary.

H. Go online to listen to *Child Prodigies* and check your comprehension.

SAY WHAT YOU THINK

A. Discuss the questions in a group.

1. The children described in Listening 2 were from the United States. Would this ever happen in your country?

2. Do you think that having some adult responsibility is good for an adolescent? Why or why not?

B. Before you watch the video, discuss the questions in a group.

1. How might a younger generation of people, called *millennials* (people born from the early 1980s through the early 2000s), view their work responsibilities differently from an older generation?

2. In your opinion, which is more important: your work life or your personal life? Which should people spend more time and energy on? Why?

C. Go online to watch a video about millennials in the workplace. Then check your comprehension.

> **the flip side** *(phr.)* a different way of looking at an idea, argument, or action
>
> **incorrigible** *(adj.)* having bad habits that cannot be changed or improved
>
> **priority** *(n.)* something that is more important than other things
>
> **punch a time clock** *(phr.)* work a conventional job with regular hours
>
> **tech-savvy** *(adj.)* knowing a lot about technology

VIDEO VOCABULARY

D. Think about the unit video, Listening 1, and Listening 2 as you discuss the questions.

1. Which of the following best determines the transition from childhood to adulthood? Why?
   a. an age (like the United Nations' age of 18)
   b. an event (like graduating, getting married, or moving into your own home)
   c. responsibilities (like caring for younger siblings or helping around the house)

2. According to the video, millennials are starting in the workforce with different experiences from previous generations. How does their transition into adulthood compare with the experiences of the children in Listening 1 and Listening 2? Which experience causes people to grow up faster? Which experience is better? Why?

Vocabulary Skill   Using the dictionary

There are many words that have similar meanings but are not exactly the same. For example, both *adolescence* and *youth* can be used for the time between childhood and adulthood. Read the following definitions.

> **ad·o·les·cence** /ˌædlˈɛsns/ *noun* [U] the time in a person's life when he or she develops from a child into an adult **SYN** PUBERTY ⟳ collocations at AGE

> **youth** ⚷ /yuθ/ *noun* (*pl.* youths /yuðz; yuθs/)
> **1** [U] the time of life when a person is young, especially the time before a child becomes an adult.

The dictionary definitions show that although the words are very similar, *adolescence* describes a more specific time period, while *youth* is more general.

Checking the definitions of similar words can help you determine which word is appropriate in a context.

All dictionary entries are from the *Oxford Advanced American Dictionary for learners of English* © Oxford University Press 2011.

A. Read the dictionary definitions of words from this unit and their synonyms. Complete each sentence with the correct word.

1. a. If you are having trouble managing your money, you should go to the

    bank to get some _____ advice.

    b. Countries such as India and China have experienced rapid

    _____ growth in recent years.

> **ec·o·nom·ic** ⚷ **AWL** /ˌɛkəˈnɑmɪk; ˌikə-/ *adj.*
> **1** [only before noun] connected with the trade, industry, and development of wealth of a country, an area, or a society: *social, economic and political issues*

> **fi·nan·cial** ⚷ **AWL** /fəˈnænʃl; faɪ-/ *adj.* [usually before noun]
> connected with money and finance: *financial services* ◆ *to give financial advice* ◆ *to be in **financial difficulties***

2. a. The lawyer can _____ that the man is guilty of the crime

    by recreating the events of the day.

   b. The report _____ us that there is still a lot of work to do.

---

dem·on·strate 🔑 **AWL** /ˈdɛmənˌstreɪt/ *verb*
1 [T] to show something clearly by giving proof or evidence: **~ that...** *These results demonstrate convincingly that our campaign is working.* ◆ **~ sth (to sb)** *Let me demonstrate to you some of the difficulties we are facing.*

show 🔑 /ʃoʊ/ *verb, noun*
● *verb* (showed, shown /ʃoʊn/ or, rarely, showed)
❯ **MAKE CLEAR 1** [T] to make something clear; to prove something: **~ (that)...** *The figures clearly show that her claims are false.* ◆ **~ sb that...** *Market research has shown us that people want quality, not just low prices.* ◆ **~ sth** *a report showing*

B. Look up the definitions of these pairs of words. Write an appropriate sentence using each word. Take turns reading your sentences to a partner.

1. assume / suppose (*v.*)

   _____

   _____

2. age / mature (*v.*)

   _____

   _____

3. response / reply (*n.*)

   _____

   _____

4. order / instruct (*v.*)

   _____

   _____

5. cover / hide (*v.*)

   _____

   _____

iQ ONLINE **C.** Go online for more practice with using the dictionary.

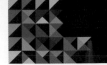

SPEAKING

At the end of this unit, you are going to present a personal story describing an important event in your life that made you feel like an adult. In order to tell your story, you will need to follow the appropriate steps for giving a presentation.

Grammar Phrasal verbs

Phrasal verbs are verbs that consist of two words used together. The first word is a verb and the second word is called a *particle*. Particles sometimes look like prepositions, but they have different meanings. The verb and the particle together make a new meaning. For example, *take on* is a phrasal verb. When you put the words *take* and *on* together, they mean "to accept."

☐   He **took on** a lot of responsibilities.

There are two kinds of phrasal verbs: *transitive* and *intransitive*.

Transitive Phrasal Verbs

A transitive phrasal verb requires a direct object.

☐   He **picked up** his brother from school.
      verb particle object

Tip for Success

In the dictionary, phrasal verbs are usually located with the definition(s) of the verb in the phrasal verb. Many dictionaries also have example sentences that follow the definitions. Example sentences are an easy way to see if a phrasal verb is *transitive* or *intransitive* and *separable* or *inseparable*.

Most transitive phrasal verbs are *separable*. This means the direct object can also go between the verb and the particle.

☐   He **picked** his brother **up** from school.
      verb   object   particle

When the direct object is a pronoun, it must go between the verb and the particle.

☐   ✓ He **picked** <u>him</u> up from school.
☐   ✗ He **picked up** <u>him</u> from school.

Some transitive phrasal verbs are inseparable. This means the direct object cannot go between the verb and the particle.

☐   ✓ My mother is busy today, so I'll **look after** the baby.
☐   ✗ My mother is busy today, so I'll **look** the baby **after**.

Intransitive Phrasal Verbs

Intransitive phrasal verbs don't take a direct object at all. They are never separable.

☐   In some situations, children **grow up** faster than in others.

It can be difficult to understand the meaning of a phrasal verb by looking at the words that make it up. Also, some phrasal verbs have more than one meaning. When you learn a new phrasal verb's meaning, you must also learn if it is transitive or intransitive and whether it is separable or inseparable.

A. Listen to the sentences with phrasal verbs. Write the particles you hear.

1. count _____

2. show _____

3. run _____ from

4. talked my son _____

5. look it _____

6. drop _____ on

B. Read the sentences. Underline each phrasal verb. Write *T* (transitive) or *I* (intransitive).

____ 1. I don't know what to do about this problem, but we need to work it out.

____ 2. I waved goodbye to my parents and got on a plane.

____ 3. It's a negotiation that continues to go on throughout childhood.

____ 4. Parentified children may feel they are giving up their childhoods.

____ 5. The child has to care for the sick parent.

____ 6. An ill mother may need help from her child because she is too ill to get out of bed.

iQ ONLINE **C.** Go online for more practice with phrasal verbs.

D. Go online for the grammar expansion.

Pronunciation | Sentence stress

Words in a sentence are not pronounced with equal stress. Words that contain important information, called **content words**, are said with more stress. They are longer, louder, higher pitched, and clearer. Words that serve a grammatical purpose are called **function words**. They are usually unstressed.

Stressing words focuses the listener's attention on the most important ideas in sentences. Using sentence stress correctly makes it easier to communicate your ideas.

Content words: usually stressed		Function words: usually unstressed	
Nouns	father, Tuesday, etc.	Articles	a, an, the
Main verbs	come, walks, etc.	Auxiliary verbs	be, have, can, etc.
Adjectives	beautiful, red, etc.	Prepositions	in, at, etc.
Adverbs	quickly, very, etc.	Personal pronouns	I, you, me, etc.
Negatives	not, can't, etc.	Possessive pronouns	my, your, his, etc.
Question words	where, how, etc.	Relative pronouns	that, which, who, etc.
Demonstrative pronouns	this, that, etc.	Short connector words	and, so, when, then, etc.

For example, listen to the following sentence. The underlined words are stressed.

I <u>became</u> an <u>adult</u> when I got <u>married</u> and <u>started</u> a <u>family</u>.

A. Listen to the sentences. Underline the stressed words you hear. Then practice saying the sentences with a partner.

1. When you become employed, you can call yourself an adult.

2. I think it's how much you can provide for yourself.

3. I think it's when you get married.

4. I think you become an adult at 16.

5. The day that I'm an adult is the day that I can do whatever I want to do.

6. The age at which you become an adult varies.

B. Underline the important content words in the conversation. Then work with a partner to read the conversation. Stress the content words.

Speaker A: Congratulations!

Speaker B: Thanks! I can't believe I've graduated already.

Speaker A: Yeah. You're an adult now!

Speaker B: But I don't feel like an adult. I still feel like a kid.

Speaker A: Really? Well, I have been taking care of my younger siblings for years now, so I feel pretty grown up.

Speaker B: I still rely on my parents a lot.

Speaker A: Well, maybe that will change now that you've graduated!

 C. Go online for more practice with sentence stress.

Speaking Skill | Giving a presentation

When you give a presentation, it is important to look and feel confident. People will be more interested in your ideas if they see that you believe in yourself and your ideas. Here are some steps to follow.

Before you give your presentation

1. Make sure you can clearly pronounce all the key words in your speech. Concentrate on proper word stress.

2. Make sure your notes are well organized. Memorize the main points of your speech so that you won't need to read your presentation. You want to look at your audience, not down at your notes.

3. Practice your presentation several times. Practice in front of a mirror and in front of a friend or family member.

When you begin your presentation

1. Introduce yourself clearly and confidently.

2. Remember to smile.

During your presentation

1. Make eye contact with members of the audience. You want them to feel you want to communicate with each of them.

2. Think about your hand gestures and posture as you speak. You want to appear relaxed and in control. If you move too much, or too little, you will appear nervous. Use gestures for emphasis and to make your points clearer.

A. Listen to a presentation about becoming an adult. Then list five suggestions you would give the speaker. Compare your suggestions with a partner.

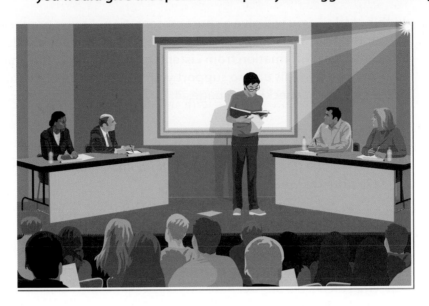

Suggestions:

1. _____

_____

2. _____

_____

3. _____

_____

4. _____

_____

5. _____

_____

B. Create a brief presentation to tell about one important event in your life. Practice the presentation once and then present it to a partner. Take note of the suggestions your partner gives you. Take turns presenting and giving suggestions.

 C. Go online for more practice giving a presentation.

UNIT OBJECTIVE ▶▶▶▶

In this section, you will give a short presentation. As you prepare your presentation, think about the Unit Question, "When does a child become an adult?" Use information from Listening 1, Listening 2, the unit video, and your work in this unit to support your presentation. Refer to the Self-Assessment checklist on page 74.

CONSIDER THE IDEAS

🔊 **A.** Listen to one person's story about the point when he became an adult. Take notes as you listen.

1. What important event became a turning point in the speaker's life?	
2. What dream did the speaker give up?	
3. How did he realize he was growing up?	

B. Work with a partner. Compare your notes and discuss the speaker's main points.

PREPARE AND SPEAK

Tip for Success

When you are brainstorming, no idea is a bad idea. Write down any ideas you have.

A. **GATHER IDEAS** Brainstorm about important events in your life that made you feel more like an adult. Make notes in the spider map.

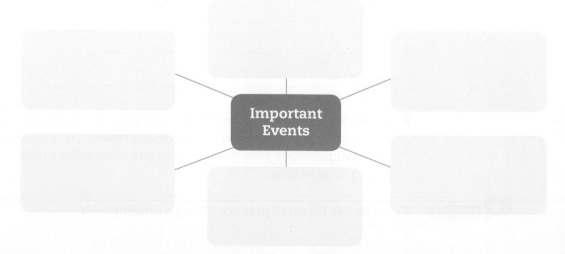

Important Events

B. ORGANIZE IDEAS **Complete these activities.**

1. Choose one event to use for your presentation.

2. Use the chart to organize your ideas. It is not necessary to write full
   sentences. Just write notes. Try to include some phrasal verbs in your
   presentation.

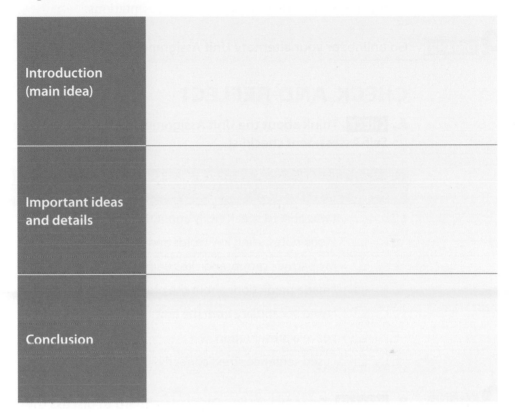

Introduction (main idea)	
Important ideas and details	
Conclusion	

3. Work with a partner to practice your presentation until you can answer *yes*
   to the following questions.
   a. Did you introduce yourself clearly?
   b. Did you pronounce all the key words correctly?
   c. Did you use stress correctly?
   d. Did you use your notes to tell your ideas rather than read them?
   e. Did you make eye contact?
   f. Did you use relaxed gestures?
   g. Did you smile?

C. **SPEAK** Present your personal story. Follow these steps. Refer to the Self-Assessment checklist below before you begin.

1. Work in a group. Take turns presenting your personal stories.

2. Pay attention to how your classmates make their presentations. Try to make predictions about what they will say. Offer suggestions to group members when they complete their presentations.

 Go online for your alternate Unit Assignment.

CHECK AND REFLECT

A. **CHECK** Think about the Unit Assignment as you complete the Self-Assessment checklist.

SELF-ASSESSMENT		
Yes	No	
☐	☐	I was able to speak easily about the topic.
☐	☐	I took notes using key words and phrases.
☐	☐	My partner, group, and class understood me.
☐	☐	I made predictions about the presentations.
☐	☐	I used vocabulary from the unit.
☐	☐	I gave a presentation.
☐	☐	I used sentence stress correctly.

 B. **REFLECT** Go to the Online Discussion Board to discuss these questions.

1. What is something new you learned in this unit?

2. Look back at the Unit Question—When does a child become an adult? Is your answer different now than when you started this unit? If yes, how is it different? Why?

TRACK YOUR SUCCESS

Circle the words you have learned in this unit.

Nouns	Adjective	Adverb
barrier 🗝	carefree	morally 🗝
burden	**Verbs**	**Phrase**
confusion 🗝	assume 🗝 **AWL**	in charge of
contradiction **AWL**	contribute 🗝 **AWL**	
frustration	pinpoint	
guidance	resent	
initiation **AWL**	reverse 🗝 **AWL**	
isolation **AWL**	run 🗝	
marker	transition 🗝 **AWL**	
milestone		
satisfaction 🗝		
sibling		

🗝 Oxford 3000™ words
AWL Academic Word List

Check (✓) the skills you learned. If you need more work on a skill, refer to the page(s) in parentheses.

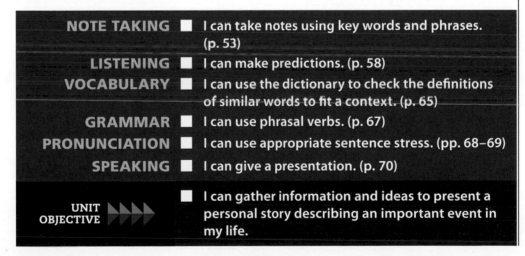

NOTE TAKING ☐	I can take notes using key words and phrases. (p. 53)
LISTENING ☐	I can make predictions. (p. 58)
VOCABULARY ☐	I can use the dictionary to check the definitions of similar words to fit a context. (p. 65)
GRAMMAR ☐	I can use phrasal verbs. (p. 67)
PRONUNCIATION ☐	I can use appropriate sentence stress. (pp. 68–69)
SPEAKING ☐	I can give a presentation. (p. 70)
UNIT OBJECTIVE ▶▶▶▶ ☐	I can gather information and ideas to present a personal story describing an important event in my life.

LISTENING	▷	making inferences
NOTE TAKING	▷	using a split page to take notes and create questions
VOCABULARY	▷	word forms
GRAMMAR	▷	present perfect and present perfect continuous
PRONUNCIATION	▷	basic intonation patterns
SPEAKING	▷	avoiding answering questions

UNIT QUESTION

Why do people do things by hand?

A Discuss these questions with your classmates.

1. What handmade products do you use on a regular basis?

2. Do you have a favorite homemade object in your house: a sweater, a blanket, or a piece of furniture or art? What do you like most about it?

3. Look at the photos. What products are being made? Why are they being made by hand?

Listen to two reports and gather information and ideas to participate in a role-play in which you present a plan for a new business.

🔊 **B** Listen to *The Q Classroom* online. Then match the ideas in the box with the students.

> a. The industrial process pollutes the environment.
> b. It becomes a hobby.
> c. ~~It's cheaper.~~
> d. People like to have unique things.

Reasons why people do things by hand	
Marcus	c. It's cheaper.
Sophy	
Yuna	
Felix	

 **C** Go to the Online Discussion Board to discuss the Unit Question with your classmates.

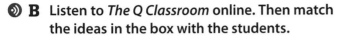

77

D Complete the survey. Which of the things below do you know how to do? Check (✓) them. Which of these do you wish you knew how to do? Put an *X* next to them.

Creating with Your Hands

- ☐ knit a sweater
- ☐ paint a house
- ☐ make a delicious meal
- ☐ build a piece of furniture
- ☐ create a designer dress
- ☐ make an origami flower
- ☐ sew a doll or teddy bear

- ☐ make a coffee mug
- ☐ make a necklace or earrings
- ☐ crochet a blanket
- ☐ make a scrapbook
- ☐ sew a quilt
- ☐ make a birdhouse from wood
- ☐ cut or style someone's hair

E Work in a group. Think about your answers in Activity D. Then discuss these questions.

1. Which of the activities can you do best? How did you learn to do it?

2. Which of the activities are things that people used to do in the past but don't often do now? Why do you think people are less interested in these activities today?

3. Which of the activities would you most like to know how to do? What would you create?

LISTENING

LISTENING 1 | Quilting's New Popularity

UNIT OBJECTIVE ▶▶▶ You are going to listen to a report describing why quilting is popular. Quilting is a craft in which pieces of fabric are sewn together to make beautiful designs. A middle layer and back are then added to turn it into a bed covering, wall hanging, or article of clothing. As you listen to the report, gather information and ideas about why people do things by hand.

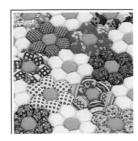

PREVIEW THE LISTENING

A. **PREVIEW** Quilting and other crafts are popular in many countries. Why do you think people like them? Check (✓) possible reasons.

☐ People have something fun and relaxing to do in their free time.
☐ People can make things exactly the way they want them.
☐ Crafts are a good way to meet others who have similar interests.
☐ People can be creative and original.
☐ It sometimes costs less to make something than to buy it.

B. **VOCABULARY** Read aloud these words from Listening 1. Check (✓) the ones you know. Use a dictionary to define any new or unknown words. Then discuss with a partner how the words will relate to the unit.

appreciation (n.)	**development** (n.) 🔑	**panel** (n.) 🔑
breed (n.) 🔑	**encounter** (n.) 🔑	**recall** (v.) 🔑
circulation (n.)	**expand** (v.) 🔑	**series** (n.) 🔑
convention (n.) 🔑	**generation** (n.) 🔑	**take note of** (phr.)

🔑 Oxford 3000™ words

 C. Go online to listen and practice your pronunciation.

WORK WITH THE LISTENING

♱ **A.** **LISTEN AND TAKE NOTES** Listen to the report about the popularity of quilting. Use the T-chart to take notes.

Reasons quilting became unpopular	Reasons quilting became popular again

B. Compare your notes with a partner. Are any of the reasons for quilting's popularity the same as the reasons you checked in Activity A of the Preview the Listening section?

♱ **C.** Read the sentences. Then listen again. Circle the correct answers.

1. Why did people stop quilting for many years?
   a. It became easier and cheaper to buy quilts instead of making them.
   b. People no longer had time to make quilts.

2. How are quilts today different from quilts in the past?
   a. Today's quilts use bits of fabric from making clothes.
   b. Today's quilts often use more exciting designs and colors.

3. How are today's quilters different from quilters of the past?
   a. They quilt for fun.
   b. They quilt out of necessity.

4. Why are businesspeople interested in crafts these days?
   a. It's an industry that is conservative and traditional.
   b. It's an industry that makes lots of money.

5. Why do teachers like their students to learn to quilt?
   a. Quilting is fun and helps students relax in their free time.
   b. Quilting helps students in lots of school subjects.

6. Why do most children not do crafts?
   a. Their families don't have time to teach children about crafts.
   b. Their families don't think that doing crafts is important.

D. Read the statements. Write *T* (true) or *F* (false). Then correct the false statements.

____ 1. A quilt can only be made by hand.

____ 2. Quilts used to be made from scraps of clothing.

____ 3. Seventy or eighty years ago, it was cheaper to buy clothes than to make them.

____ 4. Tina likes quilting because it's something she can do with her children.

____ 5. Anna wants to open a craft store because she believes she'll make a lot of money.

____ 6. In Neil Brown's experience, teenagers don't enjoy quilting.

____ 7. Quilting helps students in the classroom.

E. Discuss the questions in a group.

1. Do you think quilting will continue to be popular in the future? Why or why not?

2. What kinds of changes might cause quilting to become unpopular again?

3. Do you know of any other do-it-yourself crafts or activities that are becoming more popular?

F. VOCABULARY Here are some words from Listening 1. Complete each sentence with the correct word.

appreciation *(n.)*	convention *(n.)*	expand *(v.)*	recall *(v.)*
breed *(n.)*	development *(n.)*	generation *(n.)*	series *(n.)*
circulation *(n.)*	encounter *(n.)*	panel *(n.)*	take note of *(phr.)*

1. Larissa is on the _____ that will be discussing new trends in quilting.

2. It's been a long time since I read that book. It's hard for me to _____ some of the details.

3. Next week I'm going to a quilting _____ in New York. About 5,000 people are expected to attend.

4. Before you buy a piece of antique furniture, _____ its condition. It affects the value.

5. I bought you this gift to show my _____ of your kindness.

6. Andrea liked the first mystery book so much she decided to read all of the books in the _____.

7. It takes a special _____ of writers to understand what an audience wants and how to give it to them.

8. Robert didn't expect to run into his mean neighbor at the craft shop. The brief _____ with him made Robert upset.

9. If you look at quilts from the 1980s to today, you can see the _____ of quilting as a traditional craft to one of great energy and vitality.

10. The library never seems to have the book I want. It's always in _____. Everybody else wants to read it, too!

11. The store decided to _____ its video game section. It's now twice as big.

12. My grandfather's _____ did not grow up with TVs in their homes. People of his age often had radios.

 G. Go online for more practice with the vocabulary.

H. Go online to listen to *Bookbinding* and check your comprehension.

SAY WHAT YOU THINK

Discuss the questions in a group.

1. Why do people enjoy doing crafts? Give reasons based on your own experience or on what you heard in Listening 1.

2. Do you think schools should teach crafts to all children as part of the curriculum? Why or why not?

3. It sometimes takes weeks or months to make something by hand. How much do you think this affects a person's enthusiasm for doing crafts? Would you enjoy doing something that takes weeks or months to finish?

Listening Skill | Making inferences

We often understand ideas that the speaker has not actually stated. **Making inferences** involves "reading between the lines," or figuring out more than is actually said to understand the full meaning. Listen carefully to make inferences based on the information available to you.

In the excerpt below, the speaker, Tina, tells us about an experience at a convention.

> At this convention last year, I saw Margaret Wilson. I couldn't believe it! She has won so many awards and made so many quilts that I love. These conventions are really cool because sometimes you get to meet famous quilters.

Based on this information, we can infer that Tina has been to other conventions and that she thinks meeting a famous quilter is a very exciting experience.

Often, speakers communicate how they feel about the ideas they are presenting. To fully understand someone, listen closely to infer attitudes and emotions. Pay attention to the following.

> **Speed and pitch:** If a speaker is talking quickly, and his or her pitch goes up and down, this may indicate that the speaker is excited or passionate about the topic.
> **Tone:** Does the speaker laugh or sound serious?
> **Descriptive Words:** Listen for words that express feelings and opinions, like *love, hate, terrible, wonderful, terrific,* and so on.

A. Listen to the excerpts from Listening 1. Based on the statements in each excerpt, what can you infer? Circle the correct answers.

Excerpt 1
a. The speaker believes that quilting is important in helping students at school.
b. The speaker thinks that quilting provides a good substitute for school.

Excerpt 2
a. Tina is busy, but she's dedicated to quilting.
b. Tina doesn't have time to quilt anymore because she has children.

Excerpt 3
a. Traditional quilts were often hung on walls or used for decoration.
b. Today's quilts have different shapes and bright, non-traditional colors.

B. Listen to the excerpts from Listening 1. Circle the correct answers.

Excerpt 1

1. You can infer that the speaker is _____ .
    a. bored by quilting
    b. excited about quilting

2. Circle all the clues that helped you make this inference.
    a. his speed and pitch
    b. his tone or laughter
    c. his descriptive words

Excerpt 2

3. You can infer that the speaker is _____ .
    a. excited about the fabrics that she designs
    b. disappointed with modern quilters

4. Circle all the clues that helped you make this inference.
    a. her speed and pitch
    b. her tone or laughter
    c. her descriptive words

Tip for Success

Many tests require students to answer several inference questions. Learning to make inferences based on what you hear or read is an important part of preparing for tests.

 **C.** Go online for more practice making inferences.

A split page is a useful way to take notes and create questions about what you have listened to. To use the split-page method, divide your page into two sections by folding it lengthwise. Write your notes about main ideas and important details in the section on the right. After you have listened, read your notes and use the section on the left to write questions about what you heard. You can write down questions that are answered in your notes, questions you think might be asked on a quiz or test, or questions you would like to find answers to or even ask the speaker.

Questions	Notes on main ideas and important details

A. Listen to a presentation about building your own bicycle. Use the right side of the page to take notes about the main ideas and important details you hear.

Questions	Notes
	Reasons to build a bike:
	Difficulties in building a bike:

B. Review your notes from Activity A. Write questions about the notes in the section on the left.

 C. Go online for more practice using a split page to take notes and create questions.

LISTENING 2 | A Different Path in Life

You are going to listen to a report about a cabin designer and builder, Carl Baxter. He builds cabins and teaches teenagers, his apprentices, to build cabins, too. As you listen to the report, gather information and ideas about why people do things by hand.

A cabin in the woods

PREVIEW THE LISTENING

A. **PREVIEW** What makes some people teach apprentices to do the same thing they do? Check (✓) the things you think would motivate someone to teach an apprentice.

- ☐ Apprentices are inexpensive helpers.
- ☐ Some people truly enjoy helping the next generation to learn.
- ☐ Apprentices are excited and motivated workers.
- ☐ Businesses can use apprentice programs in their advertisements.

B. **VOCABULARY** Read aloud these words from Listening 2. Check (✓) the ones you know. Use a dictionary to define any new or unknown words. Then discuss with a partner how the words will relate to the unit.

amateur *(n.)*	**marketing** *(n.)* 🔑
apprentice *(n.)*	**operation** *(n.)* 🔑
clone *(v.)*	**overseas** *(adv.)* 🔑
gallery *(n.)*	**regard** *(v.)* 🔑
identify with *(phr. v.)* 🔑	**unique** *(adj.)* 🔑

🔑 Oxford 3000™ words

 C. Go online to listen and practice your pronunciation.

WORK WITH THE LISTENING

A. LISTEN AND TAKE NOTES Listen to the report. Take notes in the section on the right. Then read your notes and write questions about what you heard on the left.

Questions	Notes

B. Discuss the questions you wrote with a partner. Use your notes and your own ideas to answer them.

C. Read the statements. Write *T* (true) or *F* (false). Then correct the false statements.

____ 1. Carl Baxter teaches teenagers to build cabins.

____ 2. Carl Baxter's apprentices don't ever build their own cabins.

____ 3. Carl Baxter believes it's important to build cabins the way he wants, not the way the client wants.

____ 4. Carl Baxter has big plans to expand his operation.

D. Read the sentences. Then listen again. Circle the answer that best completes each statement.

1. Carl Baxter can't identify with ____.
   a. people who show teenagers how to make things
   b. teenagers who want to build cabins
   c. teenagers who watch TV all day

2. Carl Baxter learned to build cabins ____.
   a. by reading books and practicing a lot
   b. by being an apprentice himself
   c. helping others build cabins

3. Dave Black and Carl Baxter just finished a cabin for ____.
   a. a person who makes vases and bowls
   b. a famous gallery in New York
   c. a person in Japan

4. Carl Baxter loves ____.
   a. traveling overseas
   b. both cabins and the apprentices he helps
   c. dreaming of having a big operation some day

E. Based on the report, what do you think Carl Baxter is passionate about? Read the list and check (✓) the things you believe he cares about most. Then add your own ideas to the chart.

☐ Creating things others can use	☐ Living in a big city
☐ Teaching people useful skills	☐ Working with his hands
☐ Having a big business	☐ Helping people fulfill their dreams
☐ Helping others improve their own crafts	☐ Traveling around the world
☐ Designing cabins he would want to live in	☐ Educating teenagers

F. Share your answers with a partner. Discuss why you selected the answers you checked.

G. VOCABULARY Here are some words from Listening 2. Read the sentences. Then write each bold word or phrase next to the correct definition.

1. I enjoyed the book because I could **identify with** the main character. Her experiences were so similar to mine.

2. Our company spends a lot of money on advertising because we know that **marketing** is a key to success.

In Unit 3, you learned about checking the definitions of similar words to determine which word is appropriate in a context. Can you think of words that have meanings similar to *amateur*, *clone*, or *marketing*? Look up those words in a dictionary and notice how their meanings are slightly different from the words in this list.

3. My great-grandfather learned to build ships because he worked as an **apprentice** to a master shipbuilder.

4. Dickens's literature is **unique**. You'll never read other books like his.

5. I wish I could **clone** myself so that I could get all my work done. One of me is not enough to do it all.

6. Mrs. Chen's business is a growing **operation**. She just hired twenty more employees.

7. Audrey's quilts are in a show at the new **gallery** downtown that features local craftspeople.

8. I've always wanted to move **overseas** and live in a foreign country for a while.

9. Mehmet is still an **amateur**, but he hopes to develop the skills he needs to be a professional author someday.

10. I **regard** Mike as the most intelligent person I know.

a. _____ (*phr. v.*) to feel that you understand and share the feelings of somebody else

b. _____ (*v.*) to produce an exact copy of something

c. _____ (*v.*) to think of somebody or something in a particular way

d. _____ (*n.*) a young person who is trained in a set of skills, usually by a professional of an older generation

e. _____ (*n.*) the act of presenting, advertising, and selling a product

f. _____ (*n.*) a room or building for showing crafts, especially to the public

g. _____ (*n.*) a person who does an activity for enjoyment, not as a job

h. _____ (*adj.*) being the only one of its kind

i. _____ (*n.*) a business or company

j. _____ (*adv.*) in or to another country

 H. Go online for more practice with the vocabulary.

SAY WHAT YOU THINK

A. Discuss the questions in a group.

1. What do you think is the main reason Carl Baxter builds cabins?

2. Why do you think Carl Baxter loves the fact that his apprentice has started his own business?

B. Before you watch the video, discuss the questions in a group.

1. When old buildings are demolished, what do you think happens to the wood that was used to make the building? What are some ways that the wood could be reused?

2. Why do you think someone would make musical instruments out of wood from old demolished buildings?

C. Go online to watch a video about an artist who makes handmade guitars from old, used wood. Then check your comprehension.

> **VIDEO VOCABULARY**
>
> **architecture** *(n.)* the style or design of a building or buildings
>
> **developer** *(n.)* a person or company who plans new projects, such as buildings
>
> **reclaimed** *(adj.)* used for a new purpose
>
> **specimen** *(n.)* a single example of something, especially an animal or a plant
>
> **timber** *(n.)* a long, heavy piece of wood used in building a house or ship

D. Think about the unit video, Listening 1, and Listening 2 as you discuss the questions.

1. Many people enjoy making things by hand, but some people might say that learning these skills is a waste of time compared to academic study. They say that people who don't have to do these things should pay someone else to do them so they can spend their time more productively. Do you agree? Why or why not?

2. Would you be willing to pay more money for jewelry, furniture, a musical instrument, or some other object that was made by hand? Why or why not?

Vocabulary Skill | Word forms

Many words have several forms. For instance, a verb may have a noun form, an adjective form, and an adverb form. Notice all the forms of the verb *appreciate*.

Verb: I **appreciate** all the help you have given us.
Noun: We applauded to show our **appreciation**.
Adjective: It feels great to lecture to an **appreciative** audience.
Adverb: The children responded **appreciatively** when they received the gifts.

In some cases, different parts of speech of a word have the same form.

Noun: John knew that he would never forget that **encounter** with the boss.
Verb: When we arrive, I expect to **encounter** some problems.

When you look up a word in the dictionary, take note of other forms of the word. This will help you build your vocabulary. Each word form will be marked with its part of speech. Common abbreviations for *verb*, *noun*, *adjective*, and *adverb* are *v.*, *n.*, *adj.*, and *adv.*

Critical Thinking Tip

In Activity A, you have to **distinguish** between words that are related to a verb and words that are not. When you distinguish between things, you show you understand how things are different.

A. Look at verbs. Circle the word that is not a form of the verb. Use a dictionary to help you.

1. **produce** (*v.*)
   productive   prodigy   productivity

2. **inspire** (*v.*)
   inspiration   inspirational   perspire

3. **develop** (*v.*)
   deviate   development   developer

4. **operate** (*v.*)
   orate   operation   operator

5. **identify** (*v.*)
   identification   ideally   identifiable

6. **market** (*v.*)
   marker   marketing   marketable

B. Complete the sentences with the correct form of the word in parentheses. Use a dictionary to help you.

Tip for Success

When a word takes a different form, the stress pattern of the word often changes. When looking up a new form of a word in the dictionary, use the pronunciation guide to see the proper stress pattern for that form.

1. Carl Baxter is a very _____ builder. He builds five or six cabins every year. (produce, *adj.*)

2. He gets his _____ from the things customers say about themselves. (inspire, *n.*)

3. The _____ of his apprenticeship program has taken several years, but he's happy with it. (develop, *n.*)

4. Carl Baxter's _____ is small, but he believes it will grow if he finds someone who shares his vision. (operate, *n.*)

5. Carl Baxter's cabins are _____ because they all have a similar style of windows. (identify, *adj.*)

6. One of the reasons his cabins are _____ is because he hires apprentices, and customers like that. (market, *adj.*)

Preparing wood for building

 C. Go online for more practice with word forms.

SPEAKING

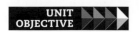

UNIT OBJECTIVE

At the end of this unit, you are going to participate in a role-play in which you present a plan for a new business that makes and sells a handmade product. During the presentation, you will need to be able to politely avoid answering questions.

Grammar	Present perfect and present perfect continuous

Present Perfect

The **present perfect** can describe actions that happened at an unspecified time in the past. The present perfect construction is *has/have* + past participle.

> Carl Baxter **has finished** another cabin.
> (He finished the cabin in the past, but we don't know when.)

The present perfect also describes actions that started in the past and continue in the present time. The words *for* and *since* are used to describe actions that started at a definite time in the past.

> She **has made** quilts **for** twenty years.
> (She started making quilts twenty years ago. She still makes them now.)
> He **has built** cabins **since** 2002.
> (He began building cabins in 2002. He still builds them now.)

The present perfect is often used to talk about past actions that happened more than once in the past.

> We**'ve seen** a lot of incredible cabins lately.
> (We saw incredible cabins several times in the recent past.)

Present Perfect Continuous

The **present perfect continuous** describes actions that started in the past, but were not finished. The present perfect continuous construction is *has/have* + *been* + present participle.

> Dave Black **has been thinking** about studying architecture in Chicago.
> (He started thinking about it in the past and is still thinking about it.)
> Yong-hwa **has been studying** there **since** last year.
> (He started studying there last year. He is still there.)
> Ahmad and his family **have been living** in New York **since** 2010.
> (The family moved there in 2010. They are still living there.)

A. Rewrite the sentences. Use the present perfect.

1. Alonzo started the project.

    <u>Alonzo has started the project.</u>

2. I thought a lot about going to design school.

    _____

3. Ellen took several architecture classes at the school.

    _____

4. Min-ju gave several small quilts to her mother.

    _____

5. There were several very good carpenters in my town.

    _____

B. Complete the conversation. Circle the correct verb form. Then practice the conversation with a partner.

Jamal: My sister Sarah and I (have gone /(have been going)) to Cathy's Craft
World on Saturdays. We (have seen / have been seeing) so much there. It's
a great store.

Ryan: I (haven't gone / haven't been going) since last winter even though
it's very close to my apartment. I walk past the store to get to work, but I
(haven't gone / haven't been going) in. I should stop in.

Jamal: Yes, you should. It's a great place. I (have taken / have been taking)
several friends there recently.

Ryan: So, what did you see there?

Jamal: Well, we (have enrolled / have been enrolling) in a class to make
chocolate truffles.

Ryan: What are chocolate truffles, exactly? I (have heard / have been hearing)
of them before, but I'm not sure what they are.

Jamal: Basically, they're round balls of chocolate with a kind of filling. Delicious!

Ryan: Wow, I ('ve never tried / 've never been trying) them, but I'd like to!

C. Go online for more practice with the present perfect and present perfect continuous.

D. Go online for the grammar expansion.

| Pronunciation | Basic intonation patterns |

Intonation Pattern

When speaking, the pitch of your voice goes up and down. This change in pitch is called an **intonation pattern**. Intonation patterns carry a lot of information. For instance, your intonation will let your listener know if you are asking a question or making a statement. It's important to use the correct intonation pattern to effectively communicate your meaning.

Rising/Falling

One of the most common intonation patterns in English is the *rising/falling* pattern, where the pitch rises and falls on the last word. This pattern is common in simple declarative sentences, direct commands, and *wh*-questions.

I enjoyed it very much.

Hand me that brush, please.

What have you seen?

Rising

For *yes/no* questions, use a *rising* pattern.

Are you concerned?

A. Listen to each sentence. Write *R* (rising intonation pattern) or *RF* (rising/falling pattern). Then repeat each sentence.

_____ 1. How much do these books cost?

_____ 2. Is the library open?

_____ 3. We're looking for the craft shop.

_____ 4. Walk north for two blocks.

_____ 5. Are you sure?

_____ 6. Please sign on the dotted line.

_____ 7. Call me tomorrow at six.

_____ 8. Have you read her new book?

B. **Listen to the conversation. Draw arrows to show the intonation patterns. Listen again and repeat. Then practice the conversation with a partner.**

Alex: Have you seen Kim's latest sculpture?

Lee: Yeah, Jae and I saw it last weekend.

Alex: What did you think of it?

Lee: It was really creative.

Alex: That's it? Come on. Tell me what you thought.

Lee: Well, I could tell she worked hard on it. But it's really not my style.

I mean, I wouldn't decorate my apartment with it.

Alex: I see. I guess we all have different tastes.

Lee: That's for sure. Did you like it?

 C. **Go online for more practice with basic intonation patterns.**

| Speaking Skill | Avoiding answering questions |

There are times when you prefer not to answer a question that someone has asked you. Here are several ways that you can avoid answering questions without being impolite.

Refuse politely.

> **A:** Who did you vote for?
> **B:** Actually, I'd prefer not to say.

Ask another question.

> **A:** Did you see the TV show *Lifeline*?
> **B:** Did you see it?

Answer a different question. You can provide related information without addressing the question that was actually asked.

> **A:** Are you looking for a new job?
> **B:** I like this job very much.

Use vague phrases. Phrases like *you might say* or *one could conclude* avoid stating your own opinion directly.

> **A:** What do you think about the new law?
> **B:** You might say it's good for some people.

Refusing politely is the simplest and most direct way to avoid answering a question. Using vague phrases is the least direct way. These strategies can be used in all types of situations.

A. Listen to the conversations. Write the strategy that each speaker uses to avoid answering a question. Then practice the conversations with a partner.

1. **A:** How old are you?

   B: I'd rather not say.

   Strategy: _____

2. **A:** What did you think of that book?

   B: You might say it gives a very unique point of view.

   Strategy: _____

3. **A:** Hello. Is Nick there?

   B: Who's calling?

   Strategy: _____

4. **A:** Is Joseph doing a good job?

   B: Joseph is a very hard worker.

   Strategy: _____

5. **A:** Can I have your address, please?

   B: I'm sorry, but I don't give out that information.

   Strategy: _____

6. **A:** Where were you on Friday?

   B: Why do you need to know?

   Strategy: _____

7. **A:** Where do you want to have dinner?

   B: Where would you like to go?

   Strategy: _____

8. **A:** How much did you pay for that car?

   B: It was affordable, and we're very happy with it.

   Strategy: _____

B. Read the questions. Write responses that avoid answer the questions directly. Then practice with a partner.

1. **A:** Why did you decide to leave that job?

   B: _____

2. **A:** What do you think of this vase?

   B: _____

3. **A:** Which quilt do you prefer?

   B: _____

4. **A:** What is your email address?

   B: _____

 C. Go online for more practice avoiding answering questions.

 **Present a business plan**

In this assignment, you are going to participate in a role-play in which you present a plan for a new business that makes and sells a handmade product. Your classmates will be potential investors in your business. As you prepare your presentation, think about the Unit Question, "Why do people do things by hand?" Use information from Listening 1, Listening 2, the unit video, and your work in this unit to support your presentation. Refer to the Self-Assessment checklist on page 100.

CONSIDER THE IDEAS

What kinds of handmade products would you be interested in making or selling? Consider the products you have heard about in this unit, the images on page 99, and any other handmade objects you can think of. Discuss these questions in a group.

1. What kinds of handmade products do you think would sell well? Why? Who would buy them?

2. Would you be willing to invest money to support someone's business that was making these products? Why or why not?

1

2

3

4

PREPARE AND SPEAK

A. **GATHER IDEAS** Read the list of questions an investor might ask an entrepreneur before lending him or her money to start a new business. Based on your discussion in the Consider the Ideas activity, add a question to each list.

<u>You and the product</u>

1. What makes the product that you are selling unique?

2. How long have you been making this product?

3. How much experience do you have running a business?

4. _____

<u>The market</u>

1. Who do you plan to sell your product to? In other words, who is your target market?

2. Who else sells products like yours? In other words, who is your competition?

3. How will you advertise and market your product?

4. _____

The deal

1. How much does it cost you to make the product, and how much will you sell it for?

2. How much money do you need or want from an investor to help you start your business?

3. How much of your profits are you willing to share with an investor?

4. _____

B. **ORGANIZE IDEAS** Choose a handmade product for which you would like to develop a business plan and get investors.

1. Prepare responses to the questions in Activity A. Are there any questions in the list you might want to avoid answering? How will you avoid answering them?

2. Think about your presentation. How will you make it interesting for potential investors (the class) and capture their attention?

C. **SPEAK** Follow these steps. Refer to the Self-Assessment checklist before you begin.

1. Present your business plan for a handmade product to potential investors (the class).

2. Answer any questions they might have, and ask them any questions you have.

 Go online for your alternate Unit Assignment.

CHECK AND REFLECT

A. **CHECK** Think about the Unit Assignment as you complete the Self-Assessment checklist.

SELF-ASSESSMENT		
Yes	No	
☐	☐	I was able to speak easily about the topic.
☐	☐	My partner, group, and class understood me.
☐	☐	I used present perfect and present perfect continuous.
☐	☐	I used vocabulary from the unit.
☐	☐	I used strategies to avoid answering questions.
☐	☐	I used correct intonation patterns.

 **B.** **REFLECT** Go to the Online Discussion Board to discuss these questions.

1. What is something new you learned in this unit?

2. Look back at the Unit Question—Why do people do things by hand? Is your answer different now than when you started this unit? If yes, how is it different? Why?

TRACK YOUR SUCCESS

Circle the words and phrases you have learned in this unit.

Nouns
amateur
appreciation AWL
apprentice
breed 🔑
circulation
convention 🔑 AWL
development 🔑
encounter 🔑 AWL
gallery
generation 🔑 AWL

marketing 🔑
operation 🔑
panel 🔑 AWL
series 🔑 AWL

Verbs
clone
expand 🔑 AWL
recall 🔑
regard 🔑

Phrasal Verb
identify with 🔑 AWL

Adjective
unique 🔑 AWL

Adverb
overseas 🔑 AWL

Phrase
take note of

🔑 Oxford 3000™ words
AWL Academic Word List

Check (✓) the skills you learned. If you need more work on a skill, refer to the page(s) in parentheses.

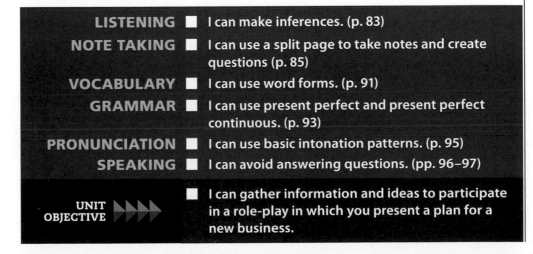

LISTENING	☐ I can make inferences. (p. 83)
NOTE TAKING	☐ I can use a split page to take notes and create questions (p. 85)
VOCABULARY	☐ I can use word forms. (p. 91)
GRAMMAR	☐ I can use present perfect and present perfect continuous. (p. 93)
PRONUNCIATION	☐ I can use basic intonation patterns. (p. 95)
SPEAKING	☐ I can avoid answering questions. (pp. 96–97)
UNIT OBJECTIVE ▶▶▶▶	☐ I can gather information and ideas to participate in a role-play in which you present a plan for a new business.

AUDIO TRACK LIST

Audio can be found in the *iQ Online* Media Center. Go to **iQOnlinePractice.com**. Click on the Media Center 🔘
Choose to stream or download ⬇ the audio file you select. Not all audio files are available for download.

AUTHORS AND CONSULTANTS

Authors

Robert Freire holds an M.A. in Applied Linguistics from Montclair State University in New Jersey. He is a teacher and materials developer with more than ten years of ELT experience. He presently teaches ESL and linguistics at Montclair State University.

Tamara Jones holds a Ph.D. in Education from the University of Sheffield in the United Kingdom. She has taught in Russia, Korea, the United Kingdom, the United States, and Belgium. She is currently an instructor at Howard Community College in Maryland. She specializes in the areas of pronunciation and conversation.

Series Consultants

ONLINE INTEGRATION

Chantal Hemmi holds an Ed.D. TEFL and is a Japan-based teacher trainer and curriculum designer. Since leaving her position as Academic Director of the British Council in Tokyo, she has been teaching at the Center for Language Education and Research at Sophia University on an EAP/CLIL program offered for undergraduates. She delivers lectures and teacher trainings throughout Japan, Indonesia, and Malaysia.

COMMUNICATIVE GRAMMAR

Nancy Schoenfeld holds an M.A. in TESOL from Biola University in La Mirada, California, and has been an English language instructor since 2000. She has taught ESL in California and Hawaii, and EFL in Thailand and Kuwait. She has also trained teachers in the United States and Indonesia. Her interests include teaching vocabulary, extensive reading, and student motivation. She is currently an English Language Instructor at Kuwait University.

WRITING

Marguerite Ann Snow holds a Ph.D. in Applied Linguistics from UCLA. She teaches in the TESOL M.A. program in the Charter College of Education at California State University, Los Angeles. She was a Fulbright scholar in Hong Kong and Cyprus. In 2006, she received the President's Distinguished Professor award at Cal State, LA. She has trained EFL teachers in Algeria, Argentina, Brazil, Egypt, Libya, Morocco, Pakistan, Peru, Spain, and Turkey. She is the author/editor of publications in the areas of integrated content, English for academic purposes, and standards for English teaching and learning. She recently served as a co-editor of *Teaching English as a Second or Foreign Language* (4th ed.).

VOCABULARY

Cheryl Boyd Zimmerman is a Professor at California State University, Fullerton. She specializes in second-language vocabulary acquisition, an area in which she is widely published. She teaches graduate courses on second-language acquisition, culture, vocabulary, and the fundamentals of TESOL and is a frequent invited speaker on topics related to vocabulary teaching and learning. She is the author of *Word Knowledge: A Vocabulary Teacher's Handbook* and Series Director of *Inside Reading*, *Inside Writing*, and *Inside Listening and Speaking*, all published by Oxford University Press.

ASSESSMENT

Lawrence J. Zwier holds an M.A. in TESL from the University of Minnesota. He is currently the Associate Director for Curriculum Development at the English Language Center at Michigan State University in East Lansing. He has taught ESL/EFL in the United States, Saudi Arabia, Malaysia, Japan, and Singapore.

HOW TO USE iQ ONLINE

iQ ONLINE extends your learning beyond the classroom. This online content is specifically designed for you! *iQ Online* gives you flexible access to essential content.

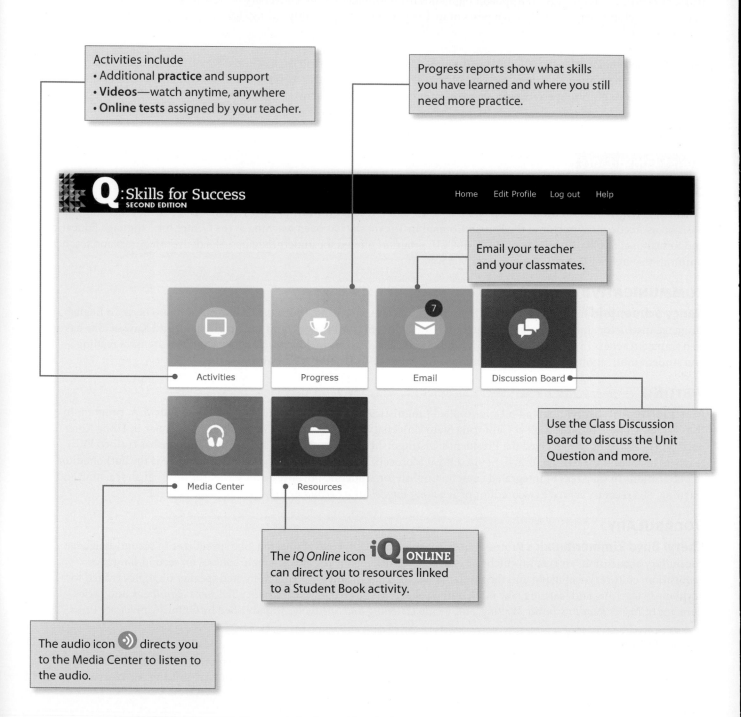

Activities include
- Additional **practice** and support
- **Videos**—watch anytime, anywhere
- **Online tests** assigned by your teacher.

Progress reports show what skills you have learned and where you still need more practice.

Email your teacher and your classmates.

Use the Class Discussion Board to discuss the Unit Question and more.

The *iQ Online* icon **iQ ONLINE** can direct you to resources linked to a Student Book activity.

The audio icon directs you to the Media Center to listen to the audio.

Q:Skills for Success SECOND EDITION

Home   Edit Profile   Log out   Help

Activities   Progress   Email   Discussion Board

Media Center   Resources

SEE THE INSIDE FRONT COVER FOR HOW TO REGISTER FOR *iQ ONLINE* FOR THE FIRST TIME.

Take Control of Your Learning

You have the choice of where and how you complete the activities. Access your activities and view your progress at any time.

Your teacher may

- assign *iQ Online* as homework,
- do the activities with you in class, or
- let you complete the activities at a pace that is right for you.

iQ Online makes it easy to access everything you need.

Set Clear Goals

STEP 1 If it is your first time, look through the site. See what learning opportunities are available.

STEP 2 The Student Book provides the framework and purpose for each online activity. Before going online, notice the goal of the exercises you are going to do.

STEP 3 Stay on top of your work, following the teacher's instructions.

STEP 4 Use *iQ Online* for review. You can use the materials any time. It is easy for you to do follow-up activities when you have missed a class or want to review.

Manage Your Progress

The activities in *iQ Online* are designed for you to work independently. You can become a confident learner by monitoring your progress and reviewing the activities at your own pace. You may already be used to working online, but if you are not, go to your teacher for guidance.

Check 'View Reports' to monitor your progress. The reports let you track your own progress at a glance. Think about your own performance and set new goals that are right for you, following the teacher's instructions.

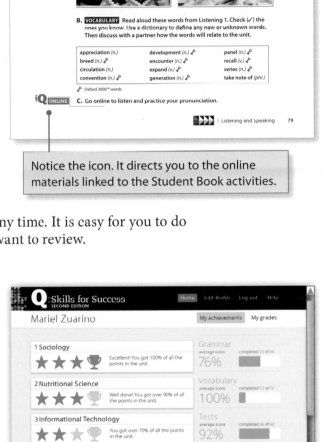

Notice the icon. It directs you to the online materials linked to the Student Book activities.

iQ Online is a research-based solution specifically designed for English language learners that extends learning beyond the classroom. I hope these steps help you make the most of this essential content.

C. n. Hemm

Chantal Hemmi, EdD TEFL
Center for Language Education and Research
Sophia University, Japan

VOCABULARY LIST AND CEFR CORRELATION

🔑 The keywords of the **Oxford 3000™** have been carefully selected by a group of language experts and experienced teachers as the words which should receive priority in vocabulary study because of their importance and usefulness.

AWL **The Academic Word List** is the most principled and widely accepted list of academic words. Averil Coxhead gathered information from academic materials across the academic disciplines to create this word list.

The Common European Framework of Reference for Languages (CEFR) provides a basic description of what language learners have to do to use language effectively. The system contains 6 reference levels: **A1, A2, B1, B2, C1, C2.** CEFR leveling provided by the Word Family Framework, created by Richard West and published by the British Council. http://www.learnenglish.org.uk/wff/

UNIT 1

acknowledge (v.) 🔑 AWL , A2
address (v.) 🔑, B2
advance (v.) 🔑, B1
aspect (n.) 🔑 AWL , A1
assess (v.) AWL , A2
capable (adj.) 🔑 AWL , B2
contact (n.) 🔑 AWL , A1
criticism (n.) 🔑, B2
effective (adj.) 🔑, A1
ethical (adj.) AWL , C1
executive (n.) 🔑, A1
exemplify (v.), C2
expert (n.) 🔑 AWL , A2
favoritism (n.), C2
issue (n.) 🔑 AWL , A1
negotiate (v.), B1
outline (v.) 🔑, B1
perspective (n.) 🔑 AWL , B1
potential (n.) 🔑 AWL , A2
staff (n.) 🔑, C1
style (n.) 🔑 AWL , B1
title (n.) 🔑, A1

UNIT 2

anecdote (n.), C2
appropriate (adj.) 🔑 AWL , A1

associate (v.) 🔑, C1
bias (n.) AWL , B2
cautious (adj.), C1
chaos (n.), B2
conduct (v.) 🔑 AWL , A2
cycle (n.) 🔑 AWL , B1
embrace (v.), B2
enthusiasm (n.) 🔑, B1
inflexible (adj.) AWL , B2
investor (n.) AWL , B1
moderately (adv.), C2
morale (n.), C1
norm (n.) AWL , B2
open-minded (adj.), C1
point out (phr. v.), B2
recognize (v.) 🔑, A1
reward (n.) 🔑, B2
stifle (v.), C2
stimulating (adj.), B2
stumble upon (phr. v.), C1
trend (n.) 🔑 AWL , A2
turn out (phr. v.), A2

UNIT 3

assume (v.) 🔑 AWL , A1
barrier (n.) 🔑, B1
burden (n.), B1

carefree (adj.), C2
confusion (n.) 🔑, B1
contradiction (n.) AWL , B2
contribute (v.) 🔑 AWL , A2
frustration (n.), B2
guidance (n.), B1
in charge of (phr.), B1
initiation (n.) AWL , C2
isolation (n.) AWL , B2
marker (n.), C2
milestone (n.), C2
morally (adv.) 🔑, C1
pinpoint (v.), C2
resent (v.), C1
reverse (v.) 🔑 AWL , B1
run (v.) 🔑, A2
satisfaction (n.) 🔑, B1
sibling (n.), C1
transition (n.) 🔑 AWL , B1

UNIT 4

amateur (n.), C1
appreciation (n.) AWL , C1
apprentice (n.), C2
breed (n.) 🔑, B2
circulation (n.), B2
clone (v.), C2

convention *(n.)* 🔑 AWL, C2

development *(n.)* 🔑, B2

encounter *(n.)* 🔑 AWL, B1

expand *(v.)* 🔑 AWL, A2

gallery *(n.)*, B1

generation *(n.)* 🔑 AWL, C1

identify with *(phr.)* 🔑, B2

marketing *(n.)* 🔑, B1

operation *(n.)* 🔑, A2

overseas *(adv.)* 🔑 AWL, C1

panel *(n.)* 🔑 AWL, B2

recall *(v.)* 🔑, A2

regard *(v.)* 🔑, A2

series *(n.)* 🔑 AWL, A1

take note of *(phr.)*, C1

unique *(adj.)* 🔑 AWL, A2

UNIT 5

adverse *(adj.)*, C1

alter *(v.)* 🔑 AWL, B1

artificial *(adj.)* 🔑, B2

commodity *(n.)* AWL, B2

compound *(v.)* AWL, C2

consist of *(phr. v.)* 🔑, A2

consume *(v.)* AWL, B1

consumer *(n.)* 🔑 AWL, A1

controversy *(n.)* AWL, B1

debate *(n.)* 🔑 AWL, A1

disturbing *(adj.)* 🔑, C1

ethics *(n.)* AWL, C1

hurdle *(n.)*, C2

identical *(adj.)* AWL, B2

modification *(n.)* AWL, B2

optimal *(adj.)*, C1

reaction *(n.)* 🔑 AWL, B1

significant *(adj.)* 🔑 AWL, A1

substantial *(adj.)* 🔑, A2

superfluous *(adj.)*, C2

trait *(n.)*, C1

ultimate *(adj.)* 🔑 AWL, B1

UNIT 6

advancement *(n.)*, C2

attitude *(n.)* 🔑 AWL, A1

career path *(n.)*, C1

climb the ladder *(phr.)*, C2

commute *(n.)* , C2

concept *(n.)* 🔑 AWL, A1

count on *(phr. v.)* , B2

currently *(adv.)* 🔑, A2

dare *(v.)* 🔑, B1

devote *(v.)* 🔑 AWL, B1

face *(v.)* 🔑, C1

figure *(v.)* 🔑, B1

log *(v.)*, C1

loyal *(adj.)* 🔑, C1

model *(n.)* 🔑, A2

particular *(adj.)* 🔑, A1

peer *(n.)*, B1

point *(n.)* 🔑, A1

radically *(adv.)*, C2

rigorous *(adj.)*, C2

serve one well *(phr.)*, C2

stable *(adj.)* 🔑 AWL, B1

stand out *(phr. v.)*, B2

structure *(n.)* 🔑 AWL, A1

UNIT 7

ache *(v.)*, B1

adhesive *(n.)*, C2

adopt *(v.)* 🔑, A2

alert *(adj.)*, C1

biological *(adj.)*, B1

deprived *(adj.)*, C1

exploit *(v.)* AWL, B1

face to face *(phr.)*, B1

flammable *(adj.)*, C1

in all probability *(phr.)*, C2

inadvertent *(adj.)*, C2

inconceivable *(adj.)* AWL, C2

interact *(v.)* AWL, B2

mandatory *(adj.)*, C1

obvious *(adj.)* 🔑 AWL, A2

odds *(n.)* AWL, B2

reunion *(n.)*, C1

synthetic *(adj.)*, C2

unreliable *(adj.)* AWL, C2

vastly *(adv.)*, C2

UNIT 8

ambition *(n.)* 🔑, B1

apex *(n.)*, C2

beneficiary *(n.)* AWL, C2

brutal *(adj.)*, C2

burnout *(n.)*, B2

collapse *(v.)* 🔑 AWL, B1

conclude *(v.)* 🔑 AWL, A2

dominate *(v.)* 🔑 AWL, B1

era *(n.)* 🔑, B1

escalate *(v.)*, C2

former *(adj.)* 🔑, A1

fundamental *(adj.)* 🔑 AWL, A2

funding *(n.)* AWL, B1

integral *(adj.)* AWL, C1

intensity *(n.)* AWL, B2

invest *(v.)* 🔑 AWL, B1

journalist *(n.)* 🔑, B1

modest *(adj.)*, B1

obsession *(n.)*, C2

reasonable *(adj.)* 🔑, A2

regret *(v.)* 🔑, B1

spectator *(n.)*, C1

ultimately *(adv.)* 🔑 AWL, B1

vulnerable *(adj.)*, B1

OXFORD
UNIVERSITY PRESS

198 Madison Avenue
New York, NY 10016 USA

Great Clarendon Street, Oxford, OX2 6DP, United Kingdom

Oxford University Press is a department of the University of Oxford.
It furthers the University's objective of excellence in research, scholarship,
and education by publishing worldwide. Oxford is a registered trade
mark of Oxford University Press in the UK and in certain other countries

Adult Content Director: Stephanie Karras

Publisher: Sharon Sargent

Managing Editor: Mariel DeKranis

Development Editor: Eric Zuarino

Head of Digital, Design, and Production: Bridget O'Lavin

Executive Art and Design Manager: Maj-Britt Hagsted

Design Project Manager: Debbie Lofaso

Content Production Manager: Julie Armstrong

Image Manager: Trisha Masterson

Image Editor: Liaht Ziskind

Production Coordinator: Brad Tucker

ISBN: 978 0 19 482075 2 Student Book 4A with iQ Online pack

ISBN: 978 0 19 482076 9 Student Book 4A as pack component

ISBN: 978 0 19 481802 5 iQ Online student website

Printed in China
This book is printed on paper from certified and well-managed sources.

ACKNOWLEDGEMENTS

*The authors and publisher are grateful to those who have given permission to
reproduce the following extracts and adaptations of copyright material:*
p. 7 from "The Best of Both Worlds?" by Tara Weiss, *Forbes,* May 23, 2007,
© 2007 Forbes LLC, www.forbes.com. All rights reserved. Used by permission
and protected by the Copyright Laws of the United States. The printing,
copying, redistribution, or retransmission of this Content without express
written permission is prohibited; p. 13 "Myths of Effective Leadership,"
from Center for Creative Leadership *Leading Effectively* Podcast, www.ccl.
org. Used by permission of Center for Creative Leadership; p. 111 "The
'Flavr Savr' Tomato Genetically Modified Food: A Growing Debate #2,"
The World at Six, July 4, 1994, http://www.cbc.ca. Copyright © Canadian
Broadcasting Corporation. All rights reserved. Used by permission of the
Canadian Broadcasting Corporation; p. 106 from "Food additives may cause
hyperactivity: study" by Maggie Fox, Reuters, September 5, 2007, © 2007
reuters.com. All rights reserved. Used by permission and protected by the
Copyright Laws of the United States. The printing, copying, redistribution
or retransmission of this Content without express written permission is
prohibited; p. 135 "'Gap Year' Before College Slowly Catches On With U.S.
Students" from CBS *The Early Show,* June 2, 2003, http://www.cbsnews.com.

Used by permission of CBS News Archives; p. 155 "The Power of Serendipity"
from CBS *Sunday Morning,* Oct. 7, 2007, http://www.cbsnews.com. Used by
permission of CBS News Archives; p. "Against All Odds, Twin Girls Reunited"
from CBS *The Early Show,* April 12, 2006, http://www.cbsnews.com. Used by
permission of CBS News Archives.

Illustrations by: p. 4 Bill Smith Group; p. 52 Claudia Carlson; p. 71 Joe Taylor;
p. 78 Bill Smith Group; p. 104 Barb Bastian; p. 128 Bill Smith Group;
p. 148 Barb Bastian; p. 180 Bill Smith Group.

*We would also like to thank the following for permission to reproduce the following
photographs:* Cover: David Pu'u/Corbis; Video Vocabulary (used throughout
the book): Oleksiy Mark/Shutterstock; p. 2 John Bohn/The Boston Globe via
Getty Images; p. 3 Ascent Xmedia/Getty Images, Trueffelpix/Shutterstock;
p. 4 Goodluz/Shutterstock (Hikers), MBI/Alamy (Meeting); p. 7 Diane Collins
and Jordan Hollender/Getty Images; p. 11 OJO Images Ltd/Alamy; p. 14 Digital
Vision/Oxford University Press; p. 20 Hugh Sitton/Corbis UK Ltd.; p. 27 Rex
Features via AP Images- Google Amsterdam. Photography: Alan Jensen,
Interior Design: D/DOCK; p. 28 White/Oxford University Press (Businessman),
Edward Frazer/Corbis UK Ltd. (Woman), Jetta Productions/Getty Images
(Mechanic); p. 29 Patti McConville/Alamy; p. 35 Cultura RM/Les and Dave
Jacobs/Getty Images; p. 36 michaeljung/Shutterstock (Woman), JGI/Tom
Grill/Getty Images (Man); p. 37 Antenna/Getty Images; p. 43 Image Source/
Oxford University Press (Casual), Stockbyte/Oxford University Press
(Formal); p. 47 paul ridsdale/Alamy; p. 51 epa european pressphoto agency
b.v./Alamy; p. 52 focal point/Shutterstock (Cap), Rebecca Photography/
Shutterstock (Cake), Cheryl A. Meyer/Shutterstock (House); p. 53 Chris
Willson/Alamy (Seijin no Hi), Blend Images/Alamy (Quinceanera); p. 60 Digital
Vision/Oxford University Press (Businessmen), Imagestate Media Partners
Limited - Impact Photos/Alamy (Boys); p. 62 Odua Images/Shutterstock;
p. 76 Atlantide Phototravel/Corbis; p. 77 Peter M. Fisher/Corbis, Happy
person/Shutterstock, dreamtimestudio/Getty Images; p. 78 Larry Lilac/
Alamy (Origami), Gallo Images/Alamy (Jewelry), Deyan Georgiev/Alamy (Bird
house); p. 79 mehmetcan/Shutterstock (Quilt); p. 78 H. Mark Weidman
Photography/Alamy (Group); p. 79 Blend Images/Alamy (Woman); p. 85 Agencja
Fotograficzna Caro/Alamy; p. 86 Kamira/Shutterstock (Tools), Mark Turner/
Getty Images (Cabin); p. 92 Dinodia Photos/Alamy; p. 94 HLPhoto/Fotolia;
p. 99 Ekkapon Sriharun/Alamy (Bag), Roberto Herrett/Alamy (Mannequin),
Juan David Ferrando/Shutterstock (Train), Marius Dragne/Alamy (Cup);
p. 102 All Canada Photos/Alamy; p. 103 Keren Su/Corbis, moodboard/Corbis
(2); p. 105 Bon Appetit/Alamy (Duck), Phanie/Alamy (Oil); p. 106 Dusan Zidar/
Shutterstock (Cereal), Image Source/Oxford University Press (Scientist),
ERproductions Ltd/Getty Images (Woman); p. 111 Jerry Horbert/Shutterstock;
p. 115 Topic Photo Agency IN/Age Fotostock; p. 119 Cris Kelly/Alamy
(Canned), Valentyn Volkov/Alamy (Fresh); p. 123 Mira/Alamy (Fresh
raspberries), Farming Today/Alamy (Moudly raspberries), Food and Drink/
Superstock Ltd. (Chicken outdoors), Michael Blann/Getty Images (Chicken
in lab); p. 127 DIZ München GmbH/Alamy; p. 128 Classic Rock Magazine/
Getty Images (Violinist), pirita/Shutterstock (Vet); p. 130 Photodisc/Getty
Images; p. 135 Neil Setchfield/Alamy; p. 141 EDHAR/Shutterstock;
p. 145 blickwinkel/Alamy (Cheetahs), Hero Images/Getty Images (Campers);
p. 152 TCI/EyeOn/UIG via Getty Images; p. 153 Science Photo Library/Alamy,
Chris Hackett/Tetra Images/Corbis; p. 154 Jim Barber/Shutterstock (X-ray),
bitt24/Shutterstock (Chips), Darkened Studio/Alamy (Dynamite), Cordelia
Molloy/Science Photo Library (Penicillin), GK Hart/Vicky Hart/Getty Images
(Microwave), Inga Nielsen/Shutterstock (Plastic); p. 155 Michael Rosenfeld/
Maximilian S/Superstock Ltd.; p. 157 Donald Erickson/Getty Images
(Cookies), Rob Walls/Alamy (Batteries), Food and drinks/Alamy (Tea),
Purestock/Alamy (Pacemaker), Stuwdamdorp/Alamy (Velcro), jennyt/
Shutterstock (GPS); p. 160 David J. Green - technology/Alamy; p. 161 Guy
Grenier/Masterfile Royalty Free; p. 162 2010 ImageForum/Getty Images
(Lascaux cave paintings), Jean-Daniel Sudres/Hemis/Corb/Corbis UK Ltd.
(Lascaux deer paintings); p. 163 Masterfile Royalty Free; p. 169 Linka A
Odom/Getty Images; p. 174 age fotostock/Superstock Ltd.; p. 179 Bob
Thomas/Getty Images; p. 180 Elvele Images Ltd/Alamy (Running), Michael
Ventura/Alamy (Tae Kwon Do), Russell Sadur/Getty Images (Soccer);
p. 181 2012 AFP/Getty Images; p. 188 Blend Images/Alamy; p. 189 PCN
Photography/Alamy; p. 190 Steve Skjold/Alamy; p. 196 Will Iredale/
Shutterstock; p. 200 Pressmaster/Shutterstock (Tennis), Eliza Snow/Getty
Images (Fencers).